SO-CAE-425

CHARLES M. LAYMON is professor emeritus, Department of Religion, Florida Southern College in Lakeland, Florida. He is a graduate of Ohio Wesleyan University (A.B.) and Boston University School of Theology (S.T.B. and Th.D.).

Dr. Laymon is the editor of *The Interpreter's One-Volume Commentary on the Bible* and the author of *The Life and Teachings of Jesus, The Lord's Prayer in Its Biblical Setting*, and *The Use of the Bible in Teaching Youth*, all published by Abingdon.

THEY DARED TO
SPEAK FOR GOD

William Jessup University
Library
333 Sunset Blvd.
Rocklin, Ca 95765

CALIFORNIA BIBLE COLLEGE LIBRARY

THEY DARED TO SPEAK FOR GOD

Charles M. Laymon

ABINGDON PRESS
Nashville   New York

22749

Copyright © 1974 by Abingdon Press

All rights reserved.
No part of this book may be reproduced in any manner whatsoever without written permission of the publisher except brief quotations embodied in critical articles or reviews. For information address Abingdon Press, Nashville, Tennessee.

Library of Congress Cataloging in Publication Data

LAYMON, CHARLES M.
They dared to speak for God.

Includes bibliographical references.
1. Bible—Criticism, interpretation, etc.
2. Bible—Biography. 3. Preaching—Biblical teaching.
I. Title.
BS511.2.L4   220.6′6   73-17196

ISBN 0-687-41649-3

Scripture quotations are from the Revised Standard Version of the Bible, copyrighted 1946, 1952, 1971 by the Division of Christian Education, National Council of Churches, and are used by permission.

MANUFACTURED BY THE PARTHENON PRESS AT
NASHVILLE, TENNESSEE, UNITED STATES OF AMERICA

This book is dedicated to the grandchildren—
Sharon, Charles Alan, Lauri, Christine,
John Brooks, Mary Beth, and John Michael
—the next generation to whom God will speak.

PREFACE

This book has been written for all who are sensitive when God speaks. It is a book for lay persons and preachers alike.

Much of the time of lay persons is spent in listening to the sermons of their preachers. In a given lifetime it will total more hours than is realized. And central in the life of the preacher is his experience in discerning and proclaiming the Word which God speaks. This is the heart of his life and ministry.

It is the purpose of this volume, therefore, to quicken this sensitivity by turning to the Bible itself, which is a deposit of hundreds of years of listening to God and speaking for God. If any persons should know what this means it is the people of the Bible and their leaders. This is what the Scriptures are all about.

Numerous questions confront us in our religious quest. When does God speak? How does God speak? How does one listen sensitively to God's Word? In what ways can man respond to what he hears? How many ways are there to communicate God's Word? Does man dare to speak for God?

No writing can shed more light on these questions than the Bible because what we meet here is not speculation but history and experience reported by a great variety of persons over a long period of time. The Bible still has the latest word in this area.

This book is not an introduction to either the Old or New Testaments. Background information was constantly needed, however, to understand the message and deeds of these persons who spoke for God. They did not live in a vacuum, hear God speak in a vacuum, or share their inspirations in a vacuum.

It was not possible to include all the leaders and preachers in the Bible, nor all the books of the Bible. The field was too large for such an undertaking. I believe, however, that the selections made are quite representative of the experience of hearing and sharing what God said to them—and to us—whether we are lay persons or clergy. What is written in this book should help us to listen more sensitively and bear our witness more dynamically—whoever we are.

The Notes (pp. 157-67) direct the reader to ideas and source materials which offer opportunity for further study in depth. I consider them an important part of this book, since they broaden the base for additional insight and understanding of its major theme.

I would be remiss if I did not express appreciation to my wife, Virginia, for being both my sounding board and typist for what is written here, and who understands the deeper spiritual meaning of these truths.

CHARLES M. LAYMON

CONTENTS

I
Who Speaks for God?

Some questions are more important than others. Little questions invite small answers, but incisive questions often lead to great answers. Asking the wrong questions may result in misleading judgments, and asking right questions in the wrong way is no less misleading.

The Ordained and Lay Ministry

The question "Who speaks for God?" is a central question, one that sends the mind in all directions for the answer. Many kinds of replies could—and should—be given. The most obvious probably would be that the ordained minister speaks for God. Most surely he does, but is this always the case when he preaches? Have you ever heard a sermon that was only the sharing of one person's private ideas and opinions with a congregation, instead of speaking for God?

Karl Barth the great Swiss theologian felt that the most precipitous and awesome moment in the life of a minister was when he stood in the pulpit and looked at the upturned faces before him as he was about to speak. What were they expecting to hear? Why did they look this way, or to him? They wanted him to speak for God. But how could he dare attempt to do this when he was only a man himself? It was an impossible situation —or was it? Can a man never speak for God?

However one would answer the above question, men and women continue to be called to speak for God. Besides the ordained ministry there is the movement of lay preaching which is growing in importance, persons not ordained who dare to believe that God can use them to communicate his word as they give their witness. At great gatherings of lay persons for study and inspiration today, nearly always there is one group which meets to discuss lay preaching. They are convinced that there are better ways of doing it than some of them are following; they want to improve their own witnessing; they desire to know just what is involved in speaking for God, for inside their being is the basic conviction that this is what they must do.

Irregular Channels of Revelation

Numerous irregular ways of speaking for God can also be found on the current scene. Night clubs, bar rooms, protest marches, dance floors, coffeehouses, and in some cases hippie pads provide the setting for communicating the Word of God. Father Malcolm Boyd, an Episcopal priest, has become the prototype of this irregular pattern in speaking for God. In the Foreword to Boyd's autobiography,[1] R. W. B. Lewis of Yale University quotes Walt Whitman in *Leaves of Grass:*

> Unscrew the locks from the doors!
> Unscrew the doors themselves from their jambs!
> . . .
> Whoever degrades another degrades me . . .
> . . .
> Through me may long dumb voices . . .
> Voices of the diseas'd and despairing, and of
> thieves and dwarfs . . . by me clarified and
> transfigured.

This is the free-flowing, down-to-earth, broad-as-mankind approach of Father Boyd, who says: "In the stages of my forty-five years I have known love and hate, anger and peace, the spirit of God and the spirits of man; I have worn many faces and masks in sad and happy dramas. Yes—in certain strangely natural and wonderful moments I have glimpsed the fragments coming together as a whole." [2] This is the way one person feels who attempts to speak for God. The pipes of God are sounding today, and the music has the timbre of a new song. And yet, is it not the same old song, sung differently at a new pitch and in new settings?

One of the most interesting phenomena of our day is the appearance of message music, both rock and folk. The young people have made much of it their own. The protest songs of Simon and Garfunkel, lyrics like "Put Your Hand in the Hand of the Man of Galilee," "God Is Beautiful," "Day by Day" from the play *Godspell,* and "I Don't Know How to Love Him," from *Jesus Christ Superstar*—all these are hauntingly reminiscent of old-time revival hymns, yet there is a difference. Theological clichés are missing here, and a new earthiness (or is it realism?) has entered the vernacular for expressing the Word. This is not church music in the traditional sense, for it came from outside the church. Yet church groups are singing it in the sanctuary, using it in processionals, and accompanying it with a guitar or a combo.

The Bible as God's Word

Traditionally the Bible has been the main source of inspiration for proclaiming the truth of God. It still is; church people have always been a people of the Book. Today we have available more translations of the Scriptures into English than ever before. The modern English version movement, beginning with Moffatt, Goodspeed, and Weymouth, has continued into the present. It was quickened by Phillips and is now kept alive by Bratcher's *Good News for Modern Man* and in the paraphrase *The Living Bible.* In addition to these, the Revised Standard Version, the New English Bible and the Jerusalem Bible have maintained the scholarly tradition of biblical versions and translations. No single century has taken as much interest in biblical readability and accuracy as the twentieth. It almost seems contradictory that this should be so when we are faced by the fact that in many ways ours is the most materialistic century of all time.

The authority of the Bible does not rest upon a dogma or doctrine; it is a fact to which each succeeding generation has borne witness. To be sure, not everyone is interested in this book and not everyone opens it regularly. Few people read it through, from cover to cover, once a year as was formerly the case, but men today cannot leave it alone. Devotional guides with daily readings have supplanted the actual reading of the Bible itself in many cases. New types of curricula in the church school have diverted the focus from Bible-centered studies. Even so, the Bible is always there, directly or indirectly. There is a steady flow of new commentaries upon it; archaeological research on biblical sites moves at a steady pace; and general books about the Bible continue to come in great numbers from the press. It remains a very lively interest.

The Bible Speaks For God

The basic reason for the centrality of the Bible in our lives is that here is a book that speaks for God. Within the words it contains there is embedded a Word that comes to life as we read it. The Holy Spirit quickens us in reading so that its biblical passages become as contemporary as if they had been written in our day. It is in the *now-ness* of its impression upon us that its authority is to be found. If men read the Bible just because the church says that they should, they would have long since given up paying attention to it, unless it spoke to them as God speaks to them. The fact is that it does speak for God, and God continues to speak in and through it. This is a fact of history.

To say that God speaks in the Scriptures is to make a tremendous claim. This is because it is not just a local tribal God that we hear speaking but the God of all the universe. It is the God

who has measured the waters in
the hollow of his hand

and marked off the heavens with
    a span,
enclosed the dust of the earth in a
    measure
and weighed the mountains in scales
and the hills in a balance.

               (Isa. 40:12)

It is the God

who stretches out the heavens like
    a curtain,
and spreads them out like a tent to
    dwell in;
who brings princes to nought,
    and makes the rulers of the earth
        as nothing.

           (Isa. 40:22*b*-23)

It is the God who is

the Lord . . . the everlasting God,
    the Creator of the ends of the
        earth.

             (Isa. 40:28)

Hearing God speak in the Bible is more than an intellectual experience; it is a personal confrontation between ourselves and God. L. Harold DeWolf has said that "of all the contents revealed by God the most important by far is God himself. There is no thought or true proposition man may know which can be compared in importance to a personal meeting with God himself." [3] This is what happens when the Bible is read with openness of heart and an eager willingness to hear God speak and to follow his will.

Men to Whom God Has Spoken

One of the main reasons that men hear God speak today as they read the Bible is that it tells the story of numerous persons to whom God has spoken in ages past. These persons, having heard God speak themselves, are able to speak for God to others, both in their own day and in ours.

Where to begin a recital of how and under what circumstances God spoke to man in the Bible is difficult to determine. The Jews customarily went back to Abraham and the covenant God made with him and through him with Israel (Gen. 17: 1-9). [4] He had an experience in which he was told that he was to be the father of "a multitude of nations" and all the land of Canaan was to be their "everlasting possession." More than this, the Lord was to be their God and at the same time, they were to be his people.

Moses also was called to serve in this same destiny by God (Yahweh), "the LORD, the God of your fathers, the God of Abraham, the God of Isaac, and the God of Jacob" (Exod. 3: 15). In a theophany he heard God speak in the midst of a burning bush, summoning him to deliver Israel from slavery in Egypt. This is the biblical explanation of the beginning of the work of Moses, including the receiving and giving of the Ten Commandments.

Centuries later the prophets were also to hear God's personal call to prophesy—Amos while tending his flocks (Amos 3:8; 7:14-15); Hosea in the midst of his marital tragedy (Hos. 1-3); Isaiah when praying in the temple, grieved over the death of King Uzziah (Isa. 6:1-13); the youthful Jeremiah at the beginning of the forty years prior to the Exile when the Hebrews were taken captive to Babylon (Jer. 1:1-12); and Ezekiel summoned by an ecstatic vision to encourage the exiles in their dark hour of servitude (Ezek. 1:1–3:27). There is no way to explain the word of the Lord as coming through these men apart from their experience of call and sense of destiny.

The record of God's speaking to men in the New Testament is no less emphatic in depicting God's personal encounter with those whom he raised up for his purpose, a purpose beginning with the covenant made with Abraham. The "word of God came to John the son of Zechariah in the wilderness" (Luke 3:2), and he went out to preach a revival that drew persons from all over Palestine to repentance and baptism. At this same religious outpouring, Jesus himself received his call to be the Messiah, being baptized by the Holy Spirit to empower him to fulfill his ministry. This was the church's understanding of the words spoken to him by God from heaven: "Thou art my beloved Son; with thee I am well pleased" (Luke 3:22).

In the early church Paul also experienced a call; he was to be an apostle to the Gentiles (Acts 9:1-22; 22:4-16; 26:9-18). In a most dramatic conversion he became transformed from a persecutor of Christians to a follower of Christ as Lord. His own explanation of what happened to him is found in Galatians where he wrote: "But when he [God] who had set me apart before I was born, and had called me through his grace, was pleased to reveal his Son to me, in order that I might preach him among the Gentiles . . ." (1:15-16). There can be no doubt that in Paul's mind God had spoken to him and that, therefore, God could speak through him to others.

Another very definite and dramatic experience of God's speaking to men in the New Testament is found in the account of how the book of Revelation came to be written. The author himself tells us that he was a prisoner on the penal island of Patmos because he had been preaching "the word of God and the testimony of Jesus." It was the "Lord's day," he says, and he was in a state of ecstasy, being "in the Spirit." A loud voice like the sound of a trumpet spoke behind him saying, "Write what you see in a book and send it to the seven churches . . ." (1:9-11). And he did.

This very cursory survey of how God spoke to men in the Bible can leave no doubt that over a period of considerably more than a thousand years, including the time before the record was put into writing, persons actually had experiences with God which convinced them that he had communicated with them, and that they were under orders from him to communicate his word and will to others. They were to be, and actually became, men who spoke for God.

What a Variety!

The persons who spoke for God throughout biblical times, and continue thus to speak to us today as we read the accounts of their work or their writings, represented a variety of personal types. Abraham was a nomad who moved from place to place with his livestock and holdings. Moses was reared in the palace of Pharaoh and possessed the canny insight of an Egyptian general. Amos was a herdsman who lived close to nature and loved outdoor life, frequently punctuating his messages with illustrations from farm and field. Isaiah was quite likely a member of the royal family who was intoxicated with the majesty of God. Jeremiah was a very sensitive man who probably associated with the life of the outer court at the temple where men congregated to study, discuss, and debate. Ezekiel was a priest, an ecstatic who was given to experiencing visions.

John the Baptist was a stern ascetic who drew apart into the wilderness to meditate where the days were hot and the nights unbearably cold. Jesus was a carpenter, loving and magnanimous in his spirit, and intense in his devotion to the will of God as he sought to carry out his mission as the Messiah. Paul was a Pharisee fanatically devoted to the keeping of the law, and just as energetically committed to taking the cause of Christ to the ends of the earth. John, the author of the book of Revelation, was, like Ezekiel, an ecstatic whose visions of judgment and the victory of Christ over all evil men and nations have held Christians for nearly twenty centuries under his spell.

In addition to these who delivered their messages orally there were the story writers of Israel to whom we owe so much for their narratives in the Pentateuch, and the historians of both Old and New Testaments who recorded religious history with the grasp of a theologian. We must add to these the psalmists who put the insights of the prophets into songs of penitence, praise, celebration, and thanksgiving, together with the wise men who spelled out the way of wisdom. And then there were the authors of the Gospels who met specific needs of their day— and ours—by telling the story of the ministry and message of Jesus.

The variety of voices represented by biblical men who spoke for God parallels the situations today in which men and women bear their witness through various channels, both within and without the church. It is clear that God has always chosen persons of many different types and backgrounds to speak for him. Today is no exception, nor is it likely that tomorrow will be any different.

Jesus had a purpose in mind when he criticized the disciples for discouraging those who cast out demons in his name, but who were not one of them (Luke 9.49-50) There is room for all and we should not too readily turn from a true word of God because it is spoken by another person who does not walk with us.

II
Narrative Writers with a Message

Everyone enjoys a story. From childhood through our adult lives narratives hold our interest, whether they are in the form of a short story or an extended novel. Human experiences, true or imaginative, capture the whole person—intellectual, emotional, and volitional—where abstract reasoning and conceptual thinking fail to move him.

Was this not the reason that Jesus cast his greatest teachings into story form and the parable became his main channel of reaching people? Matthew said that "indeed he said nothing to them without a parable" (13:34). In this way he could hold the attention of the people who gathered about him to listen, and at the same time keep those who had come to heckle quiet until he had made his point. What stories they were! His hearers could find themselves in these narratives as they identified with the Prodigal Son, the Good Samaritan, or the man who built his house on the sand.

Centuries before Jesus, the Hebrews too had their stories and storytellers, even as other ancient peoples of their day. Long before the written narratives appeared, there were storytellers who entertained and instructed the people by reciting folktales as these nomadic wanderers gathered around their campfires at night.

The entertainment factor was large in these sessions when the day's work had ended and the evening had come. There were few other sources of recreation available; adventure tales were spellbinding then even as they are now. Some of these early narrators had great skill, no doubt making picturesque use of gestures and expression that were punctuated by dramatic vocalization.

But there was more than entertainment here. Through these stories drawn from the experience of their tribe, the listeners were discovering their own identity. They could say: "We are the people who had Abraham as our father," or "We are the people whose ancestors made a covenant with Jehovah."

In particular, it was the religious interpretation which the storyteller gave to these experiences, their own and those of their ancestors, that counted most in the making of their character. Some of these interpretations came from a later time when the folktales were put into writing, but undoubtedly the meaning, God's meaning, of these experiences was a part of the original telling. W. F. Albright, the archaeologist, has said that only in this way can a nation indicate its religious and cultural history.[1] And this is what the Hebrews did.

We today must ask how much in these tales, in both oral and written form, is historical, legendary, or mythological. We think of *history*, oral or written, as a record of events as they actually occurred, *legend* as the development of an actual happening, a historical kernel, into a fuller account in line with the use to which it is to be put, and *myth* as a story that grows up apart from a specific occurrence in order to teach a truth, explain a fact of life, or provide a meaning for existence.

When one is assessing whether a story is history, legend, or myth, many factors come into play. Historical and scientific knowledge, an understanding of literary forms, the presuppositions of the biblical interpreter, and the degree of loyalty he holds to historic religious tradition—all these play a part in the final determination.

The religion of the Hebrews rested on God's revelation within the historical stream of life. It was not a philosophy or a conceptual construction apart from the events that called their nation into being. Even though Israel's faith was historically grounded, however, her religious heritage goes back into a primitive period when modern man's sharp discrimination between history, legend, and myth did not exist. But the narratives of those days, whatever their form, were taken seriously. Here the listeners found their God, their ideals, their distinctive character as a people, and their hope for the future because here their God was speaking to them.

When the Hebrews Turned to Writing

It is not realized frequently that the Hebrews were writers of history in the ancient world at least four hundred or five hundred years before Herodotus, the Greek historian who is usually thought to be the first in this field. What impulse led them to put the early folktales into writing? Probably it was a part of a developing conviction among all early peoples that things should be written down; they seemed to carry an added authority when they were expressed in writing.

This same conviction has continued to be held through the centuries. Before the printing press was invented thousands of persons had spent untold hours in writing or in copying what had been written so that it could be preserved and circulated to a wider readership. There were religious opportunities here that should not be lost. In the church, writing and copying became a religious vocation, a spiritual service performed by the monks. The written word—and later the printed word—were channels of speaking for God.

The earliest literary attempts of the Hebrews were probably poetical expressions of God's great deliverance of the nation from its enemies. One such is found in Exodus 15:1-18. It has been called a "Song of the Sea," for it tells of the experiences of the people of the covenant led by Moses as they crossed the Red Sea (Papyrus Sea or Sea of Reeds), pursued by the Egyptians, who in turn were swallowed up by the waters:

> I will sing to the Lord, for he has
>   triumphed gloriously;
> the horse and the rider he has
>   thrown into the sea. . . .
> Pharaoh's chariots and his hosts he
>   cast into the sea

And his picked officers are sunk in
the Red Sea.
                    (Exod. 15:1, 4)

The poem goes on to praise God for his "glorious deeds," and
to tell of the fear of foreign peoples who learned of this
deliverance.

Another early poem, perhaps the first extant fragment of
Hebrew literature, is the Song of Deborah in Judges 5, where
God achieves victory for the Hebrews over Sisera. This is heroic
literature of the highest order, spontaneous yet stylized. Very
ancient and very moving, it should be dated in the eleventh
(or twelfth) century B.C.:

From heaven fought the stars,
    from their courses they fought
    against Sisera.
                    (Judges 5:20)

Here is a word concerning God that the unknown poet dared
to speak, one which has brought encouragement through the
centuries to those who must struggle against adversaries.

Writers of the Pentateuch

Hebrews, followed by Christians, have regularly turned to
the writers of the Pentateuch to hear God speak. These unknown authors put into written form the folktales and other
expressions of the Hebrews. For many centuries some of these
had been recited by tribal storytellers; now a record was available of what God did and said in days past, in order to inspire
those who would read them in this new and more permanent
form. In doing this they were, as preachers, presenting their
message.

The word "Pentateuch" refers to the first five books of the
Old Testament. Sometimes this group of writings is called the

Torah. The expression "the Law" is also used as a designation for this body of written materials which formed the basis of God's revelation and was intended to be used for religious instruction.

Traditionally the Pentateuch as a whole has been assigned to Moses, and even now Bibles are published in which Genesis is called "The First Book of Moses," Exodus referred to as "The Second Book of Moses," and so forth through Deuteronomy, "The Fifth Book of Moses." This view was accepted in Judaism without question until the twelfth century A.D.[2] A close linguistic study involving literary style, thought patterns, and passage construction, however, calls for a different ascription of authorship for the Pentateuch. While one may not categorically state that Moses wrote not a single line in these five books, multiple authorship and editorial handling is a more sound conclusion. Indeed, it is all but inevitable.

It should be pointed out that nothing in the first four books of the Pentateuch claims Mosaic authorship. The fifth book, Deuteronomy, however, is designated as the memoirs of Moses and thus his authorship was also ascribed to the preceding four. Yet Deuteronomy is clearly a composite work in which there are such gaps and "proliferating cracks in its facade" as to make highly unlikely the conclusion that one person, including Moses, could have written it. Later events such as Moses' death, the conquest, and the Exile that take us beyond Moses' date are described or presupposed in this book.

Who were these writers of the Pentateuch who felt called to speak for God through literary channels? We do not know the name of a single one of them. Although they were dynamic persons with deep religious convictions and possessed by a drive to share their faith, we are left with the sole alternative of designating them by letters or general symbols.

In briefest terms we call them the Yahwist authors, the Elohist authors, the Deuteronomic editors, and the Priestly writers. The letters that are usually assigned to these persons are

J, E, D, and P. They lived in different parts of Palestine, recorded, edited, and wrote at different times, beginning around
950 B.C. and continuing until about 500 B.C. Along the way
their works were combined by editors at different stages: JE
(first half of seventh century), JED (about the middle of the
sixth century) and JEDP (probably during the fourth century).[3]

The literary history of the forming of the Pentateuch, although involved, is a fascinating story. Real people, facing
critical issues, motivated by a driving faith, and under God's
moving Spirit undertook this literary activity. They were men
called by God to reveal his character as seen in his mighty acts
to redeem man. *They were preachers, no less, who made their
witness through writing, just as men today share their testimony with pen in hand.*

The Yahwist Authors

The first and earliest strands of material as found in written
form was put down by the Yahwist or J authors. They are
called by this name because they use the word Jahveh (Yahweh)
for God. Writing at the time of the United Kingdom they are
usually dated *ca.* 950 B.C. when Solomon reigned. Although it
is likely that several authors participated in this work, there
was probably a single person who set the trend and whom we
may refer to as *the Yahwist.*

Why did the Yahwist write at this particular time? It was
during the reign of Solomon. On the surface Solomon's rule
seemed to be prosperous, but underneath there was a seamy
side marked by compromise in allowing his foreign wives to
serve their own gods. The king was also becoming secular as
he drained the country economically by a policy of forced labor
in order to complete his elaborate building projects. Everything
was being done on a grand scale; the Yahwist would also write
on an epic scale as he related the story of the nation from crea-

tion to the conquest of Canaan. He knows an account of creation, the Fall, the Flood, and God's promise to Abraham. His
literary style was moving in its perceptive characterizations as
he affirmed his faith in God. Should not Solomon and the people who were tempted by idolatry place their trust in the one
true God who bared his mighty arm in history? [4] Illustrations of
the Yahwist's writings follow.

Man and the Fall

The Yahwist view of man was that God had "breathed into
his nostrils the breath of life" after forming him out of the
dust from the ground. Thus "man became a living being"
(Gen. 2:7). The earth, in turn, was also of God's making. Did
he not plant a garden in Eden?

Man's life in the garden was to be ordered by the will of
God; he was to obey God and, if he did not, there were consequences to face. Moral responsibility existed from the outset,
and when Adam and Even disobeyed God by eating the fruit of
"the tree of the knowledge of good and evil" they had to take
the results. There was no escaping God's demand, hence from
now on there would be pain in childbirth (Gen. 3:16), weeds
to grub (Gen. 3:18), and Eden could no longer be their home
(Gen. 3:23-24).

The Yahwist insists that God made the earth with no evil
in it at the beginning; it was man's disobedience by listening to
the serpent that introduced struggle and suffering into man's
lot (Gen. 3:1-13). The steps that led to Adam and Eve's down-
fall were realistically portrayed as seeing "that the tree was good
for food, . . . a delight to the eyes, . . . and . . . was to be desired
to make one wise" (Gen. 3:6). Are these not the same ingredients in temptation today?

God, Nature, and Revelation

Our current interest in ecology would have appealed to the
Yahwist because he saw in natural events the work of God.

This is dramatically evident in his handling of the Flood story. He interpreted it as a punishment brought upon man by his evil ways: "The Lord saw that the wickedness of man was great in the earth. . . . And the Lord was sorry that he had made man. . . . So the Lord said, 'I will blot out man whom I have created from the face of the ground' " (Gen. 6:5-7). And he did—all except Noah and his family because this man was righteous and had "found favor in the eyes of the Lord" (vs. 8).

The unique insight of the Yahwist in presenting the account of the Flood is particularly evident when his story is compared with the Babylonian flood epic, known as the Babylonian Gilgamesh Epic. The accounts are similar in many ways, yet the Yahwist's high moral sensitivity dominates his telling of it. The Babylonian story is polytheistic and represents the Flood as resulting from the caprice of the gods. But the Yahwist author views it as a judgment upon the human race for sin. God and nature are related immediately; there are no secondary causes.

The Elohist Authors

Following the work of the Yahwist there was another writer (or group of writers) whom we refer to as the Elohist and whose designating symbol is the letter E. This is because he uses the word "Elohim" for God. Whereas the Yahwist probably lived and worked in Judah located in southern Palestine, the Elohist did his writing and editing during the eighth century in the northern kingdom, an area known as Ephraim. Each used the folktales and tradition of their own section and this in part accounts for their point of view. Selected illustrations of the Elohist's writings follow.

A Destiny to be Realized

In Genesis, the work of the Elohist does not appear until chapter fifteen with the call and promise made to Abraham:

"And he brought him outside and said, 'Look toward heaven, and number the stars, if you are able to number them' [what a word for the space age!]. Then he said to him, 'So shall your descendents be' " (Gen. 15:5). Here the faith of the Elohist in God's providential guidance of his people comes to the fore. There is a destiny to be realized under God's direction.

The reflected emphasis of the prophets may possibly be seen here in the Elohist's report of this promise. He was collecting and writing this material during the period of the eighth-century prophets. Amos from the south preached in the north, and Hosea from the north prophesied in his own area. Amos had a marked sense of God's work in history as he announced the coming "day of the Lord" (Amos 5:18-20), only he sees it as a time of judgment rather than of complete national blessing. Hosea also was filled with the realization of God's guidance of Israel in the past as he pictured him like a father teaching his child to walk (Hosea 11:1-3). Is it possible that the Elohist might have heard these two eloquent prophets of God? The answer must be conjectural, but their meeting is an intriguing possibility.

Trust—Not Human Sacrifice

One of the most moving narratives in the Abraham cycle which the Elohist gives is the account of Abraham's near sacrifice of Isaac, the child of promise. It is found only in the Elohist's writings. Few short stories contain the sustained tension present in this one in which Abraham is put to the test. Convinced that God wanted him to slay his young son, the patriarch sets forth to obey the command at all costs—and at what a great cost: "And Abraham took the wood of the burnt offering, and laid it on Isaac his son; and he took in his hand the fire and the knife. *So they went both of them together*" (Gen. 22:6; italics mine). Can't you see them?

When the lad asked his father where the lamb was for the

burnt offering, the old man replied: "God will provide himself the lamb for the burnt offering, my son" (vs. 8). And again there are the same words of the Elohist: *"So they went both of them together."* What poignant description! But wait, just as Abraham was about to plunge the knife into his son, whom he had bound and placed upon the altar, he heard the angel of the Lord cry out: "Abraham, Abraham! . . . Do not lay your hand on the lad or do anything to him for now I know that you fear God, seeing you have not withheld your son, your only son, from me" (Gen. 22:11-12).

Abraham—man of faith—trusted God even at the likely cost of losing his own son, child of his old age and hope of the fulfillment of God's promise. Surely the Elohist wanted to stress trust, but there may be another revelation of God beneath all this. Was not he also saying that God did not desire human sacrifice? In the very same century in which the author wrote, King Ahaz had sacrificed his son (II Kings 16:3) and Israel as a whole was accused of such practices herself (II Kings 17:17). Is it possible that by telling this story of Abraham and the child Isaac, the Elohist was also speaking for God on this subject to his own nation in that day?

Joseph and Moses

The Elohist's accounts continue here and there in the Pentateuch to the time of the conquest of Canaan. He views the experience of Joseph as an example of God's providential care for his own. When Joseph reveals himself to his brothers who had sold him as a youth into slavery, he says to them: "God sent me before you to preserve life . . . to preserve for you a remnant on earth, and to keep alive for you many survivors" (Gen. 45:5-7).

The same is true of Moses' call to deliver the Hebrews from enslavement in Egypt (Exod. 3:16-18). He was told by God to gather the elders of Israel together and to say to them: "The

Lord, the God of your fathers, the God of Abraham, of Isaac, and of Jacob has appeared to me, saying, . . . 'I promise that I will bring you up out of the affliction of Egypt, to the land of the Canaanites . . . a land flowing with milk and honey'" (Exod. 3:16-17). Again, God is a God of promise; he is a God who cares.

The Deuteronomic Authors

The book of Deuteronomy contains all of the D cycle of writings found in the Pentateuch. D does not appear in the first four books where the J, E, and P narratives intertwine. Because of the way it is written, it serves as an introduction to the historical books of the Old Testament and will therefore be considered in the next chapter in connection with these writings.

The Priestly Authors

What is the function of a priest? Briefly, the chief responsibility of a priest is to bring God to man and man to God in a life-giving relationship. How does he do this? Modern priests administer the sacraments. They are ordained for this purpose in order that the sanctity and effectiveness of the sacraments might be safeguarded. In some religious communions, the priest's effectiveness is based on the doctrine of apostolic succession. Present-day priests, however, do far more than administer the sacraments; they counsel, preach, protest, participate in public service, and engage in many community programs.

In biblical times, Hebrew priests developed a highly organized ecclesiastical system involving classes, different lines of priesthood, the office of high priest, and rules and regulations for serving in this important role. Along with this, legal proscriptions for the people were established in order to prepare them and make effective the offerings to God on their behalf. [5]

Somewhere about 500 B.C. a group of priests began to write,

edit, and prepare a strand of narratives, temple ritual, and festival observances. They had returned from exile in Babylon and were reinstating the temple system which had been temporarily disbanded due to the destruction of Jerusalem and the temple itself in 586 B.C. Now they were reorganizing; perhaps the temple had just been rebuilt (*ca.* 515). Their worship system needed to be set into motion once more.

What was the worship of God to include for the Jews following the Exile? How could it be enriched? What new meanings could be found, meanings that were implicit in the nation's own past? Such questions led the priests to turn to writing, and the priestly cycle came into being. The symbol for this group is P. Selected illustrations of the priestly authors' writings follow.

In the Beginning—God

You do not expect literary excellence in such writings as the priests prepared. Rules and regulations do not inspire eloquence. And for the most part this is true of these accounts. There is one major exception; it is the priestly narrative of creation with which the Old Testament begins: "In the beginning God . . ." (Gen. 1:1). From primordial chaos and formlessness, God called forth order: he spoke it into existence. At the very outset the writer is filled with wonder and awe as, in succession, light, the firmament, dry land, vegetation, stars and planets, creatures of the sea, air, and land appear; each in response to God's command come into existence (Gen. 1:1-25).

Finally, as the crown of creation, man is made. God said: "Let us make man in our image, after our likeness. . . . So God created man in his own image, in the image of God he created him; male and female he created them" (Gen 1:26-27). No more significant revelation concerning the nature of man could be given than this.

I have often wondered whether this creation account could possibly have been used liturgically in worship at the temple as was true of some of the psalms. There are certain lines that are repeated here and there within it, suggesting antiphonal use: "And God saw that it was good" (Gen. 1:4, 10, 12, 18, 21, 25). This evaluation reaches a climactic conclusion at the very end where the writer announces: "And God saw everything that he had made, and behold it was very good" (Gen. 1:31). Another set of repetitions are: "And there was evening and there was morning, one day" (Gen. 1:5) . . . "a second day" (1:8) . . . "a third day" (1:13) . . . "a fourth day" (1:19) . . . "a fifth day" (1:23) . . . "a sixth day" (1:31). Still another repeated expression is: "And it was so" (Gen. 1:7, 9, 11, 15, 24, 30).

What word of God in creation was the priestly author speaking? Was it not that one God, not many, created the earth and the heavens in an orderly fashion as was fitting for his divine majesty, and made man in his own image as the crown of it? [6] This prescientific epic of creation gives us once and for all the truly religious meaning of the origin of life. Not impersonal force or cosmic accident, but a purposeful act of a personal God brought the universe into existence.

God, Abraham, and the Covenant

Repetition was frequent among the authors of the Pentateuch. In numerous cases each had a tradition which another also possessed. The redactors who combined the writings usually spliced the narratives together, instead of preparing a new account based upon duplicate sources. Sometimes, however, they give both versions separately. This was true of the story of the covenant God made with Abraham. The Yahwist account is found in Gen. 15:7-21, while the Priestly account is given in Gen. 17:1-27.

We should note carefully that it was the "God Almighty" (or "God all-knowing"), as he called himself (Gen. 17:1), who inaugurated the covenant. As their superior he seemed to be forcing it upon them, but the assumption is that they too responded. In simple terms the covenant was an agreement or contract made through Abraham by which God became the God of the Hebrew people and they, in turn, became his own. It must be kept; God would at all times be true to his end of the relationship and the Hebrews must keep theirs and "walk before" God and "be blameless."

How great a God it took to bind himself to a covenant relationship with a certain specific people! It would mean that he had to keep his word, calling for an integrity that was not found in other gods. He was also an almighty or an all-knowing God. Both omnipotence and omniscience were his. The priestly authors were motivated by a tremendous conception of God. Under such inspiration the nation, just returned from exile, who read their writings or heard them read, would be strengthened to reinstate their life under the covenant.[7] And because of this same inspiration the realization that Israel was a covenant people passed, centuries later, into the Christian understanding of the new covenant through the death of Christ, who, when offering the wine, said at the Last Supper: "Drink of it, all of you; for this is my blood of the covenant, which is poured out for many for the forgiveness of sins" (Matt. 26:27-28).

God, Moses, and the Passover

Because of their responsibilities and concern for the ritual of Israel, it is not to be thought unusual that the priestly authors should have given us the account of the institution of the Passover (Exod. 12:1-20).[8] Originally this was a rite among nomads which they observed immediately prior to their departure with their flocks for the deserts of Egypt for the summer grazing. It was then given a special religious significance by the Hebrews in relation to their deliverance by God from Egypt.

The ritual as described by the priestly writers assumes that the nation was already a well organized congregation or community. Requirements were laid down which would not have been possible to follow on the eve of a swift departure into freedom. But from the standpoint of the meaning of the feast to Israel this late dating is unimportant. Ultimately it became a national feast of the Hebrews and also came to be associated with another ancient celebration, the agricultural feast of unleavened bread. Then it was taken out of the home and called for a pilgrimage to Jerusalem.

The word here is "deliverance." God had moved within history to save and establish his people. He was being true to the covenant he had made with them through Moses. When evil days came upon this people of God through the centuries—and come they did—they could look back and remember as they celebrated the Passover Feast. And because they could look back, the priestly writers wanted them to look ahead and hold firm as they anticipated the future. This is good preaching—the best.

Adam Welch of the University of Edinburgh used to say to his students that what the Passover meant to the ancient Jews as a sign and promise of God's care for his own, the Cross means to the Christian. Both here and there the constancy and integrity of God in keeping his covenant are revealed.

III
Historians Bear Witness

History deals with the near and distant past. In written form it represents a record of what people said and did. Writing history, however, involves more than a listing of events in succession. It must include motivation, causes, effects, geography, and people, and this calls for interpretation.

Modern historians subscribe to the ideal of being objective; they attempt to abstract their own feelings and reactions from the events they are describing, much as a sports commentator tries not to take sides when telecasting a game or contest. Sports commentators sometimes find it difficult to hide their partiality, however, because their tone of voice, excitement over certain plays, and admiration for specific players break through in subtle ways. We have all heard partisan sportscasters.

There is a tradition that says that Josephus, the Jewish historian who described the assault of the Romans upon Jerusalem, attempted to be all eyes and no heart as he related the account of the fall of the city. There was to be no sorrow shown. But when he stood by the side of the road in Rome and saw the victorious soldiers in parade, carrying the sacred relics from the temple they had destroyed, Josephus could not hold in any longer. He cried aloud in agony. Yes, the historian has feelings too, and it is sometimes difficult for him to be objective.

Biblical Historians

The historical books of the Old Testament, *broadly speaking*, include Joshua, Judges, Ruth, I and II Samuel (originally one book), I and II Kings (originally one book), I and II Chronicles (originally one book), Ezra, Nehemiah, and Esther.[1] The authors, or groups of authors, were men who cared about the events they were describing. These not only dealt with the beginnings and early development of their own religion, but also met a need in the Hebrew community at the very time they were writing. More than this, these historians had a stake in the outcome of the events they were describing.

The question may be raised as to how one can be certain of the historical accuracy of these accounts since the writers had a personal concern in the happenings they were recording. But there is a counter question that should also be interjected. Had they not had some personal involvement in the history of Israel would they have possessed the kind of insight that was necessary to put together the historical data meaningfully and intelligently? History includes many subtle and subjective elements, and only one who writes from the inside can really *tell all the truth.*

So-called neutral criticism is all but impossible to achieve in recording history, although it may be approximated. But even if it were fully possible, would the results be satisfactory? G. Ernest Wright points to Carl Sandburg's *Lincoln* as an example of the personal identification of an author with his subject producing a classic: "A full, rich, far better [than neutral] history is . . . Carl Sandburg's *Lincoln,* where the author insofar as possible relives and participates in every facet of Lincoln's life, identifies with and absorbs himself in Lincoln." [2] The historical writers of the Bible do this very same thing with the story they are telling.

Salvation History

The biblical historians speak for God. This is their unique character as authors. In *Heroes and Hero-Worship,* Carlyle wrote that: "No great man lives in vain. The history of the world is but the biography of great men." [3]

As men write history today in the field of the social sciences, they deal with human causes and effects. All the relationships—economic, political, environmental, geographical, ecological, and sociological—are brought to bear upon the human event. The evolutionary principle of growth and development is dominant in the telling of the story, although the suddenness of change is also included. This approach is proper for their province.

The biblical historian deals in human relationships likewise; his characters are very human and walk on feet of clay. He depicts the succession of events like beads on a string, layed out on a horizontal plane. But he does more than this; God is also seen as a vertical factor in the developing story. In fact he invades life at every point as the chief figure in the drama of destiny. History is in his hands and its final outcome under his control. Paul Tillich summarizes this perspective in these words: "Here it is obvious that God reveals himself not only *in* history but also *through* history as a whole. The gods of space are overcome; history has a beginning, a center, and an end." [4]

Because the biblical historians take this view they are essentially proclaimers of the Word of God. In their portrayal of the values of being good and doing good, they move beyond the field of ethical culture and include the purposes of God and the reality of sin and forgiveness as demonstrated in history. In this they become preachers who speak for God because the history they write is theologically oriented. It is the *message* of the events that they record which concerns them finally.

Why Historical Writings?

The Hebrews turned to writing history because their God had had a part in making history. Man also had a role in the shaping of events. It was man and God together within the fabric of time who participated in a divine-human engagement. This was too important not to record.

Historical interest among the Hebrews became particularly acute during the reign of Solomon. By this time the nation had come into being and had actually made history; there was something to write about and there were early sources at hand to use, such as the Court History of David as found in II Samuel 9–20, and I Kings 1–2. Here the writers moved beyond narratives which included, besides history, legends and myths, and began to write as historians would write. They did not have at hand the tools of a modern historian that would enable them to distinguish between primary, secondary, and tertiary strands in their sources. But they were responsible authors, even so, who were selective although not critical in the handling of their materials.

Deuteronomy and the Historical Writings

Who wrote and edited the historical books of the Old Testament? Their identity, as far as their personal names are concerned, is unknown. But we can learn much about them through a close study of what they wrote. As a result of such study the authors and editors of Joshua, Judges, I and II Samuel, and I and II Kings are called the Deuteronomic historians, because in their handling of the story of Israel they followed the principles of the D writer or writers in Deuteronomy.

In connection with the book of Deuteronomy there is a most dramatic set of circumstances. A book of the law was discovered by Hilkiah the priest in the temple at Jerusalem in 622 (II Kings 22:8-23:35). This book formed the nucleus of Deuteronomy (5-28). King Josiah was much impressed and made it the basis of a tremendous religious reformation in the nation. Since it purported to be three addresses of Moses it carried great authority.

How the book got into the temple and who wrote it, it is impossible finally to say. Just when it was written is also a matter of conjecture. As an undercover writing, the material in it may have been in preparation in priestly circles for many decades, edited and brought to light at this particular time. What is of prime importance, however, is not this set of circumstances but the fact that it was written and became the basis for a religious reform. Its authors were daring to speak for God.

The book of Deuteronomy was committed to the importance of a single sanctuary for the nation. Moses is represented as saying: "Take heed that you do not offer your burnt offerings at every place that you see; but at the place which the Lord will choose . . ." (Deut. 12:13-14). On the basis of this injunction, the main emphasis in the reform movement of Josiah became the centering of worship in the temple at Jerusalem. Local sanctuaries and shrines throughout the nation were to be abolishished. These had been corrupted by neighboring superstitions, immoralities of Baal worship, and such practices as divination. Worship must be purified at all costs.

There were also other specific emphases in Deuteronomy which not only sparked the reforms of Josiah, but also provided perspectives which influenced the point of view in the historical writings. God's rewarding of the righteous and his punishment of the evil was one of these. Another was God's loyalty to his promises. Still another was the Deuteronomist's interest in chronology as he placed the events in the life of the nation in sequence. This suggests the stream of history concept.

Underlying these emphases is the basic idea that history is important to both God and man. God is active in its making, and man is held responsible for the way he lives. Thus the historian who writes within this perspective cannot be a secular person if he is to take into account *all* the elements in the picture; his calling is religious as he interprets human events. Some illustrations follow.

The Covenant at Shechem

The covenant was of utmost importance to Abraham and Moses. It also became pivotal to Joshua in the reaffirming of the covenant relation between God and the nation at Shechem (Josh. 24:1-28). [5] As a final act before his death Joshua, who had succeeded Moses, "gathered all the tribes of Israel to

Shechem." The elders, the heads, the judges, and the officers of Israel "presented themselves before God," and Joshua spoke for God to the people.

What happened at Shechem? Joshua gave them a recital of major events in Israel's history, going back to Terah, the father of Abraham. Isaac, Jacob, and Esau were then mentioned in succession as recipients of God's guidance and blessing. The contribution of Moses and Aaron, and the deliverance from Egypt were indicated next. Finally there was a summary of the conquest of Canaan under Joshua in which God had given Israel victory over its neighboring peoples.

In all this, Joshua was interpreting sacred history and a "ceremony of covenanting" took place between God and Israel. An important part of this ceremony was a spelling out of the requirements of the covenant (Josh. 24: 14-15). Loyalty to God was central; all other gods must be rejected. In response, the people joined in with an affirmation of allegiance: "We . . . will serve the Lord, for he is our God " (vs. 18).

Joshua then turned to the problems they would face in serving the Lord (24:19-20), but the people replied in a new declaration of their determination to do so: "Nay; but we will serve the Lord. . . . the Lord our God we will serve, and his voice we will obey" (24:21, 24). Finally "a great stone" was set up as a witness to the covenant made between God and the people that day.[6] They had reaffirmed their loyalty to God.

The value of such public reaffirmation of one's faith, then and now, is great. It keeps men from taking their religion for granted. Each generation must make the religion of the past a present reality by reaffirming it. And individuals, likewise, find a deepening experience as they reassert their original allegiance to God from time to time. Halford E. Luccock, in an unpublished sermon, put it poignantly when he said: "Even in Babylon the faithful children of Israel renewed their souls in memory of the distant heights of Jerusalem." [7] Was this not what Israel was doing in reaffirming the covenant at Shechem? She was looking both back and up—and forward.

A Philosophy of History in Judges

Throughout the centuries mankind has looked for a philosophy of history that would interpret the course of human events. If only a formula could be found that would explain what has happened in the past, is now taking place, and is yet to occur, understanding might be possible. A better future could perhaps be assured if we knew what makes things turn out as they do and have done in the past.

The ancient Greeks found their formula of history in the idea that there is a cycle of events which is repeated over and over again. Backgrounds may alter and outward appearances look different from what they had been, but there is really no basic difference. Change is illusory in the cyclical new. Progress is not possible on this basis, for the future is, in principle, predetermined to complete the circle.

In our day the application of the evolutionary view of the development of life has been widely used in understanding numerous areas of experience. Beginning as a biological principle, it was quickly taken over into the social fields so that we now speak of the evolution of government, the family, and public institutions. Even history has been interpreted in terms of the evolutionary principles of growth and ordered change.

A third approach to history, one with which we are familiar in modern society, is that held by communism. Karl Marx enunciated it, taking his cue from the philosophy of Hegel. This philosopher interpreted life—and history—as moving from one extreme (thesis) to another (antithesis). Finally it rested midway (synthesis) between the other two. According to this formula the goals of history are predetermined. The communists applied it to the economic aspects of history in particular, and concluded that on the basis of economic determinism the communization of the world was inevitable. In this picture revolution was also to play a part.

The history writer, or writers, who gave us the book of Judges had a formula for history too. This has been called the "cycles of apostasy" view. Israel would sin and as a result be handed over to a foreign power. Then she would repent and God would send a leader to deliver the nation. But again she would sin and again be enslaved by her enemies. In all this, God was at work, calling the plays; he was ultimately and immediately in control of history. For this reason the cycles of apostasy view of history might be regarded as a theology of history.

The brief summary of events in Israel's life found in Judges 2:11-23 illustrates this understanding of history. It tells how the people "did what was evil in the sight of the Lord and served the Baals; and they forsook the Lord, the God of their fathers, who had brought them out of the land of Egypt" (2:11-12). With what consequences? "So the anger of the Lord was kindled against Israel, and he gave them over to plunderers" (2:14). In the sorry plight that followed, God took pity on them, sending them judges to guide and deliver them. So again the people became loyal to God, "but whenever the judge died, they turned back and behaved worse than their fathers" (2:18-19).[8]

An Illustration in the Gideon Account

The story of Gideon illustrates this sequence. His prowess, wholehearted spirit, and courage against the Midianites who were oppressing Israel has long held the interest of biblical readers. The account of his leadership as a judge opens with the words: "The people of Israel did what was evil in the sight of the Lord; and the Lord gave them into the hand of Midian seven years" (Judg. 6:1).[9] Then the people "cried for help to the Lord" (6:6), and God, in turn, sent them Gideon to deliver them, saying to him: "Go in this might of yours [the Lord's] and deliver Israel from the hand of Midian; do not I send you?" (vs. 14).

How Gideon tricked the Midianites with only three-hundred men carrying trumpets, jars, and torches is one of the great sagas of antiquity. His slogan was: "For the Lord and for Gideon" (7:18). At the close of his rule over Israel, he died, a man of wealth and many wives. But "as soon as Gideon died, the people of Israel turned again and played the harlot after the Baals . . ." (8:33). And the cycle began all over again.

The historian who wrote this and other accounts in Judges was, in essence, preaching a sermon on sin, forgiveness, and redemption. History, in his view, was morally conditioned. He was as interested in asserting this truth as he was in recording events.

Toward Becoming a Nation

When the Hebrews moved into Canaan the tribes scattered and settled in different sections of the country. They were thus surrounded by foreign neighbors. Although the idealized account of the conquest of Canaan in Judges 1:1–2:5, similar to the description in Joshua, pictures the Hebrews as steadily moving northward from the south en masse, the records, as we saw in the Gideon account, indicate that the tribes were spread about like islands surrounded by the Canaanites, who were often hostile.

From time to time the tribes would come to one another's aid; again they would refuse to do so. The Song of Deborah, in Judges 5, is very outspoken at this point, condemning some (Reuben, Gilead, Dan, Asher) who refused to help and praising others who did (Ephraim, Benjamin, Manasseh). A people was finding itself, as well as a place for itself in the Promised Land. Only later, under King Saul and King David, did this people achieve national unity, along with securing their own land where they might live as a nation. The story of how this took place was written by the historians in Samuel and Kings.

Since the Hebrews were the people with whom God had

made a covenant, the putting of the story into writing was a proclamation of the Word of God, no less; it was a great religious event, this making of the monarchy whereby tribal groups were united and became a nation ruled, under God, by a king. The historians who wrote about these things were actually speaking for God. Their motivation was as religious as that of the minister who preaches his heart out.

IV
Historians Interpret the Monarchy

There are two accounts of the anointing of a king to rule over Israel in I Samuel, representing different religious points of view. One sees the request for a king as an act of rebellion against God.[1] Only after persistent demand did Samuel, the last of the judges and the first of the prophets, yield to public urging and anoint Saul (I Sam. 8:1-22). Samuel warned the people what was in store for them if they were to have a king. This account is based upon a late source and lists specific losses that would follow (8:9-18). They sound as though they are based on experience. Could they reflect the problems of the people under Solomon at the very time when the traditions were being collected? God, said Samuel, regarded this request for a king as a rejection of his rule over the nation, but he finally acceded to it saying "Hearken to their voice, and make them a king" (8:22).

The second point of view which is found in an earlier source (I Sam. 9:1–10:16) represented God as favoring the kingship. He voluntarily says to Samuel: "Tomorrow about this time I will send to you a man from the land of Benjamin, and you shall anoint him to be prince over my people" (9:16). Thus Saul, son of Kish, was anointed. On this occasion Samuel said: "And you shall reign over the people of the Lord" (10:1). Even though Saul would be king, he was to rule for God. We call this a theocracy. In our own nation, traditionally, we have embraced this same view. It became very evident when the words "under God " were inserted in our national pledge to the flag. For this new task the author says that Saul was given "another heart" (10:9). He would need it to rule under current circumstances.

In the above the writing of what is an ostensibly political history turns out to be a thesis in religious understanding of the function and responsibilities of government. Each historian here, whether in favor of or against the monarchy, is writing to present his point of view *as a proclaimer of the word of God;* he is identifying with what he writes because for him it carries a message.

The Breakdown of Saul

Saul was a heroic, yet a tragic figure. Towering head and shoulders above his peers, he was a gifted leader and a successful soldier. No doubt at first in his battles with the people of Canaan he was spurred on by the "new heart" which he had been given at his anointing. In time, however, war seemed to make him less sensitive to God's voice and will.

On one occasion Saul had been told by Samuel to fight a holy war against the Amalekites; he was to kill them off—man, woman, infant, suckling, ox, sheep, camel, and ass (I Sam. 15: 3). The D editor does not pause, as we would have done, to consider the ethics of such a command. He centers on what he regards as the real issue, namely, obedience to God. You will remember that this was one of the main points of emphasis by the D historians. Saul was victorious, but he did not obey this command; he saved Agag the king and a considerable number of cattle.

When confronted by Samuel, who had heard the bleating of the sheep and the lowing of the oxen, Saul skirted the truth, claiming that the animals had been saved *by the people* for sacrifical offerings to God. How religious! How untrue! But Samuel would listen to no excuses for disobeying God. He personally hacked Agag in pieces "before the Lord" (I Sam. 15:33), and told Saul: "You have rejected the word of the Lord, and the Lord has rejected you from being king over Israel " (15:26). Samuel and Saul then parted forever.

Our moral sensitivity recoils at much in this account, which, however, should be read and evaluated in terms of the mores of that day. The D historian is affirming that obedience is everything. Thus when Saul disobeyed, both God and Samuel turned away from the king. As a result his personality began to disintegrate, seemingly becoming schizophrenic. Clearly he developed a persecution complex and homicidal tendencies. The historian sees this as God's judgment on one who disobeyed. [2] Even man's mental life is morally conditioned. Here the historian speaks for God.

Behind the historian's interpretation of Saul's saving of the cattle for sacrifice—even though this probably was not a reason but an excuse—we may possibly see the struggle between the cultic and the prophetic views. The prophetic outlook puts obedience first; the cultic places ritualistic practices in the foreground. Had Samuel been a priest, and the author a priestly editor, he might have viewed Saul's disobedience differently.

The Preeminence of David

Of all the kings in Israel's history none has found such a high place in the life of the nation as David. As a youth he was the Robin Hood of the young monarchy as he darted in and out among its neighbors and by strategy and strength overcame its enemies. His friendship for Jonathan, the son of King Saul, and his loyalty to the king, even when Saul was trying to kill him, mark him as a heroic figure.[3] He was the first to give the new nation a major capital city on the heights of Jebus, captured from the Jebusites, which he named Jerusalem.[4] In his enthusiasm he carried the ark of the covenant into Jerusalem, thus reviving an ancient focal point for trust in God. Even though he did not get to build the temple, he layed the groundwork for this center of the nation's worship. Intrigue and struggle dogged his days to the very end, but his impression upon the nation was so great that as men looked toward the future, they spoke of the Messiah who was to come as "the son of David."

The David stories affirm the conviction that he was God's choice for fulfilling his purpose in the life of his people. Not only did he choose him, but he also gave him strength to act in the making of the nation. Few biblical "biographies" are more completely centered in the idea of the direct action of God in personal life than the story of David. An illustration follows.

David's Sin, Judgment, and Forgiveness

We have already noted that one of the earliest and best sources used by the historians who recorded the story of David in Samuel and Kings was The Court History of David, found in II Samuel 9–20, and I Kings 1–2.[5] In this source a marked degree of objectivity may be found. Was the writer himself an eyewitness of the events he describes? Did he get his material from eyewitnesses? He was not as obvious in his preaching as some of the later historians in the Bible, but he did consistently affirm that God was active in history, in the lives of persons through whom he worked, as well as in national events.

A story in the Court History of David that particularly carries moral and spiritual implications is the account of David's sin against Uriah the Hittite when he lay with his wife Bathsheba and thus violated their marriage (II Sam. 11:1–12:25). The writer's daring frankness in recording the sin of such a famous person as King David is a tribute to his honesty. He is not writing a gossip column, but history with a religious interpretation; he is speaking for God.

David was attracted to Bathsheba as he saw her bathing in the courtyard of her home. Evidently she lived near and below the palace. Her husband, Uriah, was a Hittite who as a mercenary soldier was in David's employ, at present fighting the Ammonites at Rabbah. King David exercised his royal prerogative and brought Bathsheba into the palace. When she became pregnant, he called her husband home on the pretext of securing information concerning the fighting, but hoping that he would be united to his wife. Thus he could claim that Uriah was the father of the child she was carrying. But Uriah kept the strict continence that was required of a soldier, so the plan was not successful. Consequently David arranged that he should be placed in a dangerous area in the battle and, as anticipated, he was killed.

Then David married Bathsheba and she bore him a son. At this point in the narrative the historian writes: "But the thing that David had done displeased the Lord" (II Sam. 11:27). By inserting such a comment the historian becomes a preacher. He dares to speak for God.

Subsequent events bear out God's action in history. First Nathan the prophet came to David and accused him (12:7-12), predicting dire results because of his sin. And David repented saying: "I have sinned against the Lord" (12:13). Second, Nathan told David that the child would die. The king was in anguish over the prospect and by prayer and fasting sought to avert the child's death. But death came, and the historian notes that David "arose from the earth, and washed, and anointed himself, and changed his clothes; and he went into the house of the Lord, and worshiped" (12:20).[6] He had accepted God's judgment upon him. After this, Bathsheba conceived again, and the child who was born was Solomon, who succeeded David on the throne.

There is more to this account than meets the eye. A deep religious sermonic teaching lies beneath the events as they are presented. They say that no king in Israel is to regard himself as the sole judge of his own acts. God's will is the final element in every decision.

The death of the first child born to David and Bathsheba may possibly have suggested God's turning from the king. On the other hand, the birth of Solomon could, in the same vein, be regarded as a renewal of the relationship between God and David. This line of thinking carries a message.

Solomon's Prayer
at the Dedication of the Temple

At its height the temple was a focal point of the worship, ideas, and ideals of the Hebrew people. What was David's dream became Solomon's accomplishment. As the account of its building is related in I Kings (6:1–7:51) there is a feeling of excitement and piety in every detail. The record culminates in a description of its dedication and, particularly, in the dedicatory prayer of Solomon (8:22-53). The spirit and editorial contribution of the D editors pervades this record in Kings. They selected what to them were the important traditions and fashioned them to have certain emphases. These unknown (by name) persons were preachers and teachers who spoke for God.

The prayer of King Solomon is outstanding in its religious philosophy and teachings as it illustrates the outlook of the book of Deuteronomy. This prayer as presented should probably be regarded as a composition of the Deuteronomist, containing appropriate petitions for such an occasion as the dedication of the temple. This does not mean that Solomon was not a man of prayer and that such ideas as the prayer of dedication contains were completely foreign to him. What is important here is that a great faith in God, in his providential care for his own, in his demand for obedience, and in his punishment of sinners is declared in no uncertain terms at the dedication of the temple.[7] How appropriate! It is not unlike dedicatory rituals today when the Christian faith finds liturgical expression.

The prayer opens with an address to God: "O Lord, God of Israel, there is no God like thee, in heaven above or on earth beneath, keeping covenant and showing steadfast love to thy servants who walk before thee with all their heart" (I Kings 8: 23). Reference is then made to David (he is still pivotal) and the promises God made to him with the petition: "O God of Israel, let thy word be confirmed, which thou hast spoken to thy servant David my father" (vs. 26).

Before the prayer closes, special cases requiring strength and forgiveness are mentioned. These include sinning against one's neighbor (vss. 31-32), drought (vss. 35-36), famine, and pestilence (vss. 37-40). From first to last there is a summons here to take God seriously. History is uttering a divine word.

The Chronicler Speaks for God

Even though the identity of the authors of the Pentateuch and the Deuteronomic historians is unknown, they exerted a tremendous influence in both interpreting and proclaiming the faith of Israel. Many biblical readers peruse the accounts these persons have written and follow the narrative with interest, but miss their religious drive and contribution to the Hebrew faith. They are far more than recorders of events, for they are, through their historical writings, preachers of the Word.

There is yet another historical author whom we refer to as the Chronicler. We know that he wrote considerably after the historians we have been following, because he records events and their meaning whose date is as far down the line as 400 b.c. Some would place the figure even later.[8] He opens his work of telling the story of Israel with a lengthy genealogical account (I Chron. 1–9) that begins with Adam and ends with the death of Saul. The rule of David next commands his attention (I Chron. 11–29) because he regards him as the moving force behind the temple, even being responsible for the religious offices necessary for its operation.

In II Chronicles the Chronicler tells of the reign of Solomon, the divided kingdom—Israel and especially Judah—and the Exile in Babylon. The Chronicler then continues his history to include the return of the Jews from Babylon with the rebuilding of the walls of Jerusalem as well as the temple, and the reestablishment of the law. These events are depicted in the books of Ezra and Nehemiah.

What about the religion of the Chronicler? What teaching message or truths of God was he attempting to affirm and communicate as he wrote his history? Why does he retell so much of the story already covered by the D historians? In what way does he speak for God?

The Chronicler was a man of great and marked convictions. He was certain that God wanted him to recount the history of the nation from a particular stance. There were basic religious ideas that he felt called upon to stress, and this is exactly what he did. He was addressing his own day as he wrote of past events.

Among the Chronicler's concerns was to emphasize the life of the nation after the Exile, when its religion was expressed through priests, the temple, and the law. Its national identity was being reestablished constituting it a holy congregation. All this he saw as a development of what David (not Solomon) had begun. As we have noted he regarded him as the true originator of the temple, its staff, and its system. The Levites along with the temple procedures interested him especially. Could he himself have been a Levite and a singer in the restored temple?

Two Illustrations
The Dedication of the New Temple

What was Israel without a temple? Its religious life through the centuries had come to center in this House of God, and when it was destroyed by the Babylonians under Nebuchadnezzar in 586, the hearts of the people were faint. It was difficult at best to be marched as exiles to Babylon, but it was doubly tragic to think of the temple itself in ruins. This feeling of desolation is reflected in Psalm 137 when the Israelites' captors demanded that they sing one of the songs of Zion, probably a song sung in the temple worship. The psalmist asked in sorrow: "How shall we sing the Lord's song in a foreign land? " (vs. 4).

The Jews began to trek back to Jerusalem under Sheshbazzar, following the edict of Cyrus the Persian who had conquered Babylon in 539 without even a battle. It was not a mass movement, by any means. Some were too aged to return, and others did not wish to do so. There was an abortive attempt to rebuild the temple after they arrived which did not succeed. Only under Zerubbabel, who led a well planned venture back to Jerusalem sometime before 522, was the task of rebuilding it begun once more about 520. Two prophets of the period, Haggai (1:1-15), and Zechariah (4:8-10) promoted the project, which was completed about 515.

Just as the temple built by Solomon was dedicated, so the new Temple constructed by Zerubbabel was also consecrated to the service of God.[9] In the latter case there was far less lavish ceremony with fewer animals sacrificed. More emphasis, however, was here placed upon meeting requirements for the priests and Levites, including their courses or divisions: "And they set the priests in their divisions and the Levites in their courses, for the service of God at Jerusalem . . ." (Ezra 6:18). Now the priests and Levites would be ceremonially clean to celebrate the feasts of the Passover and the Unleavened Bread, which they immediately did as a culmination of the dedication (6:19-22).

This was no perfunctory celebration but one that was deeply moving and joyful. During the Exile holding such services had been impossible, but now with the new temple and the consecrated religious functionaries, the Jews were once more able to celebrate their national heritage and be ceremonially united to their God in forgiveness and loyalty. The Chronicler, true to his interest in rites and ceremonies, commented upon this experience by saying: "And they kept the feast of unleavened bread seven days *with joy; for the Lord had made them joyful*" (Ezra 6:22; italics mine). God was present in the ceremonies of the temple! The Chronicler speaks this word for God.

The Reaffirming of the Law

There was another aspect to the religion of the Jews in addition to the ceremonial practices which centered in the services of the temple. This was the sacred place that was given to the law. These two continued side by side, sometimes complementing each other and again competing.

When the Hebrews returned to Jerusalem, they not only reestablished the temple ritual and the ceremonial feasts, but also reaffirmed the law as the basic legislation for regulating their life. The Chronicler tells in his most dramatic form how Ezra the scribe (priest) read the law from a wooden pulpit to all the people assembled in the square before the Water Gate (Neh. 8:1-12). The people stood from early morning until midday.

How moving is the Chronicler's account! It says: "And Ezra opened the book in the sight of all the people; . . . and when he opened it all the people stood. And Ezra blessed the Lord, the great God; and all the people answered, 'Amen, Amen,' lifting up their hands; and they bowed their heads and worshiped the Lord with their faces to the ground " (8:5-6). The people were also helped to understand what was read, for the sense was explained clearly to them (vs. 8). This was necessary because Ezra read the law in Hebrew and the people spoke Aramaic, the everyday speech of the masses.

The law that was being read was probably certain portions of the Pentateuch.[10] It was called "the book of the law of Moses," and the Chronicler notes that this was the book "which the Lord had given to Israel" (Neh. 8:1). Already the Pentateuch had come to be regarded as inspired, a gift from God. Editors had combined P with J E D in about 410, and Ezra had brought it to Jerusalem in about 397. It was then accepted as the constitution of the Jewish state.

The Chronicler regards the occasion of the reading "the book of the law of Moses" as a time when the people were touched to the quick with feelings of guilt. But Ezra urged rejoicing instead of mourning and weeping: "This day is holy to the Lord your God; do not mourn or weep . . . do not be grieved, for the joy of the Lord is your strength" (Neh. 8:9-10). We are to see here not only Ezra's message to the people, but also the Chronicler's. There were to follow a celebration of the Feast of Booths, a public confession of sin, and a renewal of the covenant (8:13–10:39). *Now their future was in God's keeping. This was the message the Chronicler left to the nation as he completed his history.*

V
Prophets Preach the Word

We have been seeing how biblical narratives and biblical historians not only record the tradition of the Hebrews but also interpret it. The final emphasis is upon what it means. In this sense the narrators and historians were preachers of the Word. The Hebrews felt this way about them, and in the Jewish canon, Joshua, Judges, I and II Samuel, and I and II Kings are called the Former Prophets; historical writings become prophetic documents. This is because history is viewed as an act of God, and a record of these events is therefore theological and sermonic.

A Direct Line to God

The prophets had immediate communication with God. These men were unusually sensitive to what he wanted to say to the nation. This sensitivity was so highly developed that they could speak to the people as though God himself were addressing them. Frequently among their utterances are scattered such phrases as: "Thus says the Lord" (Amos 1:3); "Therefore the Lord says" (Isa. 1:24); "Thus says the Lord of hosts" (Zech. 8:9).

Even more important than these expressions is the fact that the prophets customarily spoke in the first person for God, as though their words were his words and his words were theirs. Take this passage from the opening sermonic summary in Isaiah (1:1-31). It contains a series of oracles against Judah, which had been rebelling against God, and uses such phrasing as: "I have had enough of burnt offerings of rams" (vs. 11); "even though you make many prayers, I will not listen" (vs. 15); "I will turn my hand against you" (vs. 25). This could be duplicated in passage after passage throughout the prophetic books.

This was a unique and central element in the prophetic consciousness. Even the apostle Paul did not dare to speak for God in the first person. He believed that he knew the mind of Christ as he wrote, stating on one occasion: "Now concerning the unmarried, I have no command of the Lord, but *I give my opinion as one who by the Lord's mercy is trustworthy*" (I Cor. 7:25; italics mine). Most preachers today would take their stand with Paul; few, if any, would attempt to speak for God in the first person as the prophets did.

The prophets were not always accepted on these terms. Amos could say: "Surely the Lord God does nothing, without revealing his secret to his servants the prophets" (3:7), but Israel did not share his conviction wholly. It might be said that the Hebrews as a people never accepted a single prophet. Kings sometimes consulted them, often to turn away and follow their own inclinations. Centuries later Jesus himself referred to this disbelief of the nation. As he approached Jerusalem for the last time he cried out: "O Jerusalem, Jerusalem, killing the prophet and stoning those who are sent to you!" (Matt. 23:37). He too was to receive the same treatment before the week had ended.

Regardless of their lack of acceptance, and it was tragic, the prophets through the centuries stand out as figures carved in rock. Time only serves to enlarge their greatness. Mankind has found it impossible to bypass their moral and ethical pronouncements. Whenever they are read and pondered, the conscience of mankind is sharpened.[1]

Called to Prophecy

The prophets appeared in Israel over a time span of about six-hundred years, beginning from the middle of the eighth century, when Amos received his call. They continued to be prominent into the period of the Exile with both the named and unnamed prophets of that time. After the return from Babylon their appearance and activity diminished.[2]

How does one explain the beginning of the prophetic movement itself and the conviction of the prophets that they spoke for God? In the first instance it would seem that God himself raised up this movement, for that is what it was. In this same vein we could ask how does one account for Pentecost, the zeal and activities of the reformers in the time of Luther, or the great revival movements under Wesley? The New Testament speaks of these as "times of refreshing . . . from the presence of the Lord " (Acts 3:19). What better answer could be given?

The conviction of the prophets that they spoke for God is made plausible by the accounts they give of their call into this ministry. Amos, Hosea, Isaiah, Jeremiah, Ezekiel, and others include a record of this event. It was their validation, their sheepskin, and their ordination, all wrapped into one. They were not self-appointed, mercenary preachers, as Amos was driven to say when Amaziah the priest at Bethel advised him to go home, where his message would be more readily accepted and his material returns greater. Amos struck back with: "I am no prophet, nor a prophet's son; but I am a herdsman, and a dresser of sycamore trees, and the Lord took me from following the flock, and the Lord said to me, 'Go, prophesy to my people Israel' " (7:14-15). Just what happened to Amos at the time of his call is a matter of conjecture. Was it the coming to a head of a growing conviction, or what has been called a "convulsive moment" ?

Isaiah's experience of summons to the prophetic ministry is carefully described in chapter 6 of his writings.[3] Distraught over the death of the good king Uzziah, the prophet had gone into the temple to pray. While he was in prayer or meditation it seemed that the ceiling of the temple had been lifted, and its walls pushed back so that the prophet found himself in the throne room of heaven. He is thrust into a feeling of unworthiness by the vision of the Lord "sitting upon a throne, high and lifted up" (6:1). As the seraphim called to each other, "Holy, holy, holy is the Lord of hosts; the whole earth is full of his glory," Isaiah cried out: "Woe is me! For I am lost; for I am a man of unclean lips . . ." (vs. 5). He had seen the Lord and by contrast felt unclean. Immediately there was an experience of forgiveness as one of the seraphim took a burning coal from the altar, touched his lips and said: "Behold, this has touched your lips; your guilt is taken away, and your sin forgiven" (vs. 7). It was then that the prophet could hear God's question: "Whom shall I send, and who will go for us?" And Isaiah responded: "Here am I! Send me" (vs. 8).

The ingredients of a prophetic summons are all here—a feeling of need, a vision of the glory and holiness of God, a sense of sin, an experience of forgiveness, and a call to prophesy. These are the universal elements in all summonses to preach, then and now. They may be present in different settings, through different means, and in different words; but here is the classic pattern of content.

From that moment Isaiah began a ministry that lasted forty years intoxicated with the majesty of God. He went forth not inspired by an inner psychic, mantic power of divination as non-Israelitic seers believed a prophet should be, but because God had spoken to him. Yehezkel Kaufmann emphasized this by saying: "The prophet does not share in a special divine mantic faculty. He does no more than announce the 'secret' that the sovereign and ominiscent God has revealed to him." [4] On this basis the foundation of prophecy is a gift of grace.

Great Truths Cast in Great Words

The prophets did not lack for words. Phrases pour forth from their lips in torrents of eloquence, yet containing a moral drive that is not lost in wordiness.

Listen to Amos refer to God as

> he who made the Pleiades and Orion,
>   and turns deep darkness into the
>   morning,
>   and darkens the day into night,

> who calls for the waters of the sea,
>   and pours them out upon the
>   surface of the earth.
>   (5:8)

Hosea speaks in aphorisms when he says:

> For they sow the wind,
>   and they shall reap the whirlwind.
>   (8:7)

Jeremiah writes with poetic verve:

> The Lord will roar from on high,
>   and from his holy habitation
>   utter his voice;
> he will roar mightily against his fold,
>   and shout, like those who tread
>   grapes,
> against all the inhabitants of the
>   earth.
>   (25:30)

Perhaps the most majestic writing of all is to be found in the prophecies of II Isaiah, who promised the return of the Jews from exile. Such passages as the following are typical:

> Have you not known? Have you not
>   heard?
> The Lord is the everlasting God,
>   the Creator of the ends of the earth.
> He does not faint or grow weary,
>   his understanding is unsearchable.
> He gives power to the faint,
>   and to him who has no might he
>   increases strength.
> Even youths shall faint and be weary,
>   and young men shall fall exhausted;

but they who wait for the Lord
shall renew their strength,
they shall mount up with wings like eagles,
they shall run and not be weary,
they shall walk and not faint.

(Isa. 40:28-31)

An interesting study has been made of the speech forms in the prophetic books. Just as in sermons today we single out certain types, such as the expository sermon and the topical sermon, the prophetic utterances can be classified. This need not mean that the prophets were always conscious of making certain literary distinctions according to type, but that their statements turned out this way because of the varied purposes of their utterances. Three forms of speech were used. The first, according to Westermann, were accounts or narratives; the second were prophetic speeches to individual persons, the people of Israel, and the other nations; the third were utterances between man and God, a kind of prayer. These speech forms lent themselves to woes, parables, laments, curses, and judgments.[5]

On occasion the prophets acted out their messages. Each time they were seen, whether or not they spoke, they were prophesying. For instance, when Isaiah wanted to warn Egypt of her near capture by the Assyrians he walked about unclothed as a slave for three years. His nudity (he wore only a loincloth) said more to them and to Judah than many words (Isa. 20:2 ff). Another illustration of such demonstrative action is found in Jeremiah's wearing a yoke of iron (Jer. 28:10). It was to show the prophet's conviction that God had sent the yoke of Babylon upon the nation. Jeremiah also took a waistcloth he had worn and buried it in the bank of the Euphrates. Days later he dug it up in a state of decay. This is the way the ruin of Judah will be, he said (Jer. 13:1-11). And Ezekiel in Babylon once packed an exile's baggage to announce that the Jews would one day return from Babylon (12:1-7).[6]

A Call for Purity in Worship

The prophets took the worship of the Lord seriously. It was a question not of proper or improper liturgy, but of sincerity in prayer and praise that concerned them most. When the Hebrews first entered Palestine after the wilderness wanderings they settled among the Canaanites where the worship of the local gods, the baalim, was practiced. These were fertility cults involving immorality in the very act of worshiping their gods. In order to get a heavy crop or numerous calves and lambs, it was felt that the baal who presided over these must be served. The God of Mt. Sinai seemed far away, and the local baalim were near at hand. Did Jehovah actually have any jurisdiction over such practical needs of the people? Had they not left him behind when they came into Canaan? These questions were typical of the ones which the people asked.

Such practical considerations were very real to some of the Hebrews, and many turned to baal worship as a pragmatic thing to do. Thus the stream of worship became polluted, and for several hundred years the prophets sought to purify it. Sometimes the people actually turned to baal worship as such and forgot their God. Again, they continued to worship Jehovah, but introduced practices from baal worship into their own religion; they worshiped their God in a heathenish fashion. We call this interpenetration of one religion with that of surrounding faiths *syncretism*. It has been a constant threat on the Christian mission field. Why not adjust, adapt, and conform? What harm will follow?

The preaching of the prophets never fell into vague generalities; it was directed toward definite targets. This maybe seen in their messages against baal worship.

Hosea is very specific as he cries out against the involvement of the people in these fertility cults:

> Therefore your daughters play the harlot,
> and your brides commit adultery.

> I will not punish your daughters when they play the
>   harlot,
>   nor your brides when they commit adultery;
> for the men themselves go aside with harlots,
>   and sacrifice with cult prostitutes,
> and a people without understanding shall come to ruin.
>
> (4:13c-14)

There will be no double standard in this judgment; men and women will be punished alike. Such outspoken language in preaching would be regarded today as offensive, but the prophet spelled it out in no uncertain terms.

Idol worship was also an ever-present problem in this situation, for the baal was frequently represented by a bull:

> And now they sin more and more,
>   and make for themselves molten
>   images,
> idols skillfully made of their silver,
>   all of them the work of craftsmen.
> Sacrifice to these, they say.
>   Men kiss calves!
>
> (Hos. 13:2)

The problem in idol worship is that the idol is always less than what it is intended to signify, hence it stands in the way of the god it represents. The Hebrews took a firm stand against idol worship, not only in the Ten Commandments where the making of graven images was forbidden, but also in the sarcasm which prophets like Isaiah poured out upon idolatry. He pictures the process involved in making an idol in which the tree out of which the idol is made is also used for firewood to warm the body and to cook the food: "And the rest [what is left over after using part of the wood for personal needs] of it he makes into a god, his idol; and falls down to it and worships it; he prays to it and says, 'Deliver me, for thou art my god!'" (Isa. 44:17).

The final thrust of the prophets in their attempt to purify worship was to strike out against the substitution of religious ceremony for ethical conduct. This is a danger whenever men tend to overemphasize liturgy at the expense of social consciousness. The prophets would not approve of attempts to save the world by substituting ritual for godly action. Listen to this sermonic pronouncement of Isaiah against empty forms of worship:

> Bring no more vain offerings;
>   incense is an abomination to me.
> New moon and sabbath and the calling of
>   assemblies—
>   I cannot endure iniquity and solemn assembly.
> Your new moons and your appointed feasts
>   my soul hates;
> they have become as burden to me,
>   I am weary of bearing them.
>
> (1:13-14)

Instead of so much ceremony which had blinded their vision of human need, Isaiah presented God's call to repent:

> . . . remove the evil of your doings
>   from before my eyes;
> cease to do evil,
>   learn to do good;
> seek justice,
>   correct oppression;
> defend the fatherless,
>   plead for the widow.
>
> (1:16b-17)

There is a sense of urgency present in this prophetic message that is characteristic of all great preaching. An issue is at stake, but, more important, the lives of persons are at stake.

Justice for All

In the prophets, justice between man and man is an expression of the righteousness of God. At the core of their preaching is the burning conviction that a righteous God demands justice as his children relate themselves to one another. It is difficult to explain their sensitivity to injustice on any other basis than this; it is theological, but it is also warm and personal. Good theology is always of this character if it really speaks for God. A theology that does not cause a man to be stirred within when face to face with injustice is academic only; God is not present. It is no accident that the great social prophet of this century, Walter Rauschenbush, wrote a book which he titled *Theology for the Social Gospel.*

The classic statement in all the prophets on the necessity for justice is one that Amos made when he cried out with fervor: ". . . let justice roll down like waters, and righteousness like an everflowing stream" (5:24). This demand was to offset the emptiness and artificiality of conventional worship. Solemn assemblies, burnt offerings, cereal offerings, and peace offerings were an abomination to God. Even the dulcet music of the harp had turned into noise (5:21-23).

Hosea has a similar word, one which Jesus himself used, in which he says: "For I desire steadfast love and not sacrifice, the knowledge of God, rather than burnt offerings" (6:6). Jesus was being criticzed because he cared for outcasts and sinners who were being unjustly treated by official Judaism. In replying he called upon his opponents to "learn what this means," and then gave them the above words from Hosea.

There is another succinct statement, this one from Micah, which is in the same vein:

> He has showed you, O man, what is good;
> and what does the Lord require of you

> but to do justice, and to love kindness,
> and to walk humbly with your God?
>
> (6:8)

Notice how the emphasis is placed upon action. They are to *do* justice, to *love* mercy, and to *walk* humbly.[7]

The prophets do more than proclaim general truths on the need for justice. In their preaching they undergird their message with references to specific cases of injustice. Amos speaks of oppressing the poor and crushing the needy (4:1); he knows that there is little justice in the courts and that profiteering is practiced in the grain market (5:10-13); even the needy were being sold into slavery by their creditors if they owed as little as the cost of a pair of shoes and could not pay (2:6). And Isaiah singles out the practices of the rich in grabbing up the land from the poor, joining house to house and field to field until there was no more room (5:8). Hosea even includes the advantages which the priests were taking of the people; they were growing wealthy in the practice of their rites; "they feed on the sin of my people" (4:8).

God's Role in History

In the Preface to *An Historian's Approach to Religion,* Arnold Toynbee explained how he came to write on this subject. He offered it to the University of Edinburgh for the Gifford Lectures, as he says, "because, in my own life, I had reached a point at which the question 'What is our attitude towards Religion?' was calling for an answer too insistently for me to be able to ignore it any longer. . . . I believe . . . that, in finding myself pursued by this question, I am having one of the characteristic experiences of the living generation in the Western World."[8] Toynbee is convinced that the meaning of the universe is the question that historians should seek to answer.[9]

Long before Toynbee, the prophets of Israel were certain that the God of all the universe was working out his purposes in history, and that its meanings and significance lay in this very fact. They theologized history just as the historical writers of their nation had done.[10] It was God's story just as truly as man's, even more so, because he had the first and the last word.

What preacher in our time would dare to stand up in his pulpit and interpret current events in the light of God's action? Who among us would have pointed to the specifics of the war and peace in Vietnam and said, "Thus says the LORD"? I am not referring to the practice of identifying current events with apocalyptic passages in Daniel or the book of Revelation. That is another matter. Instead, I am thinking of identifying the immediate decisions of God in relation to what is happening in history today.

It is one thing to say that currently where there is evil, God is working for goodness, where there is hatred, God is striving for love, and where there is injustice, God is moving toward justice. But it is another thing to say, as II Isaiah did, that God caused the Babylonians to capture Jerusalem and to enslave the people as a punishment for their sins. And that now that their punishment was sufficient, God would lead them back to their homeland (40:1-5). More than this, he would accomplish such a feat by using Cyrus the Persian conqueror who, for this purpose was his "servant," although he did not worship him (45:1-4).

Why was God in a position to do this? Isaiah gives the answer to this question:

> I am the Lord, and there is no other,
>   besides me there is no God;
>   I gird you [Cyrus], though you do not
>   know me,
> that men may know, from the rising
>   of the sun
> and from the west, that there is
>   none besides me;

I am the Lord, and there is no
other.
I form light and create darkness,
I make weal and create woe,
I am the Lord, who do all these
things.

(45:5-7)

God is the Lord of nature and history. In the final analysis there are no secondary causes. Besides him "there is no other."

In this line of thinking Isaiah is one with the historians of Israel who interpreted the events in the life of the nation as due to the direct action of God. It was he who called Abraham and established the covenant; it was he who delivered the Hebrews from Egypt and instituted the Passover; it was he who gave the Commandments in the wilderness; it was he who overcame the Canaanites, giving to his people their own place in the sun; it was he who was both king-maker and king-breaker; it was he who caused Sennacherib to break camp and return overnight to Assyria without conquering Jerusalem, even though he had surrounded the city so that she was like a bird in a cage.

No Foreign Alliances

Because the prophets were convinced that God was in control of history they opposed all foreign alliances. The security of the nation lay in putting its trust in God who would act on their behalf if they remained faithful. For this reason Hosea did not favor the making of alliances with Egypt and Assyria: "Ephraim is like a dove," he said, "silly and without sense, calling to Egypt, going to Assyria" (7:11). Each alliance was intended to offset the other in a power politics play. And in this same vein Isaiah urged king Ahaz not to make an alliance with Assyria to protect them against the coalition between Syria and Israel which was threatening Judah. His advice to the king was: "Take heed, be quiet, do not fear, and do not let your heart be faint . . ." (Isa. 7:4). But the temptation to play politics was too great for Ahaz, and he made the agreement in spite of the prophet.

The political astuteness of the prophets is one of the amazing phenomena of the ancient world. Their advice was seldom taken, and sometimes they were regarded by their peers as foreign agents because what they advocated was so unpopular. When Jeremiah said to Zedekiah, king of Judah, "Serve the king of Babylon and live" (27:17), he appeared to be very unpatriotic. But the enemy was about to take the city of Jerusalem; resistance would destroy it, their home life, and their institutions. Submission would have meant a foreign governor, but they could have kept their basic institutions intact. The king, however, would not listen, and destruction with exile followed in 586 B.C.

It should not be forgotten that in all this the prophets were not political leaders, but religious seers, speaking for God. They were like Thomas Jefferson, who said at one point in our history: "Indeed, I tremble for my country when I reflect that God is just." [11] When preachers of our day include matters of government in their preaching it is sometimes regarded as out of order for a man of the cloth. It has been said that Pastor Niemöller once passed on to Hitler the concern of the church over certain events in Germany. The Führer replied: "You look after the church and leave such things to me." The prophets were at the opposite pole from this point of view, as was Niemöller.

The Day of the Lord

It is characteristic of the human mind to set goals toward which men and nations are moving. Men, therefore, receive with hope and enthusiasm the preaching of the prophets that history will culminate in the Day of the Lord. Traditionally it was interpreted as a time when the nation Israel would triumph over all her enemies and rule victoriously. It was primarily God's own victory, for his purpose in history would at last be realized.

There was more, however, than a military victory in the coming of the Day of the Lord. The prophets saw it as a time of judgment when Israel herself would be held accountable to God. Amos, who was the first of the prophets to use this title for the kingdom, firmly stressed its moral nature. He warned the nation because of its sins and said:

> Woe to you who desire the day of the Lord!
> Why would you have the day of the Lord?
> It is darkness, and not light; . . .
> Is not the day of the Lord darkness, and not light,
> and gloom with no brightness in it?
>
> (5:18-20)

On a brighter side the Day of the Lord was also to be a time of blessing. Peace (Isa. 2:4; 11:6-9), the renewal of nature (Isa. 55:13; 60:13), and the creation of a New Eden were a part of the outlook.[11] Isaiah pictures such a time when he speaks for God, saying:

> For behold, I create new heavens and a new earth;
> and the former things shall not be remembered
>   or come into mind
> But be glad and rejoice for ever in that
>   which I create;
> for behold, I create Jerusalem a rejoicing
>   and her people a joy.
> I will rejoice in Jerusalem, and be glad in my
>   people;
> no more shall be heard in it the sound
>   of weeping
>   and the cry of distress.
>
> (65:17-19)

There was always a tendency in Israel for some to consider the Day of the Lord as their own special privilege. This view was not acceptable to such a prophet as Isaiah; they had a world mission to fulfill:

> I am the Lord, I have called you in righteousness
>   I have taken you by the hand and kept you;
> I have given you as a covenant to the people,
>   a light to the nations.
>
> (42:6)

What a theme for preaching! But this was not all that Isaiah grasped as the Word of God for his day—and for the future. World peace would be a reality as nations would come to Jerusalem to learn the law and return to their homes to fulfill it. Then they could "beat their swords into plowshares, and their spears into pruning hooks" (2:2-4).

The future likewise was to be the age of the Messiah when one would come as God's viceroy on earth to bring justice, peace, and understanding. Then, as Isaiah said, the earth would be "full of the knowledge of the Lord as the waters cover the sea" (11:1-9).

It remained for another prophet to add a crowning touch to the prophetic message for the future. Joel is sometimes forgotten among the giants of the prophets, yet the Word God gave him to utter as he envisioned the future may have been among the greatest of all. Peter used this Word to interpret Pentecost:

> And it shall come to pass afterward,
>   that I will pour out my spirit on all flesh;
> your sons and your daughters shall prophesy,
>   your old men shall dream dreams,
>   and your young men shall see visions.
> Even upon the menservants and maidservants
>   in those days, I will pour out my spirit.
>
> (2:28-29)

Here the living presence of God in the Spirit, without whom no prophet can speak and no preacher can preach, is promised.

VI
Psalmists Sing of God and Man

Martin Luther said of the Psalms: "There you look into the hearts of all the saints as into a beautiful gay garden, indeed as into heaven; and in that garden you see spring up lovely, bright, charming flowers, flowers of all sorts of beautiful and joyous thoughts about God and his mercy . . . and the very best thing is that *they speak such words about God and to God.*" [1]

These words were written more than four hundred years ago; and as we read them and the Psalms today, we cannot but conclude that the great reformer is expressing our feelings too. The Psalter is truly the flower garden of the Scriptures. And just as blossoms send forth a fragrance that lifts our spirits, so the Psalms used in private worship or public praise both teach and inspire us. They preach the truth as they tell of God's way with man and man's search and discovery of God.

What Is a Psalm?

The obvious answer to this question is that a psalm is a poem. It has poetic form and expresses truth in ways that often escape other types of writing. How better can praise to God be uttered than when the psalmist says:

> Praise the Lord!
> O give thanks to the Lord, for he is good;
>   for his steadfast love endures for ever!
>
> (106:1)

Take another example; when one is moved by the beneficent mercy of God and wants to put his sentiments into words, can he say what he feels more directly and warmly than in the statement which opens Psalm 103?

Bless the Lord, O my soul;
  and all that is within me, bless his holy name!
Bless the Lord, O my soul,
  and forget not all his benefits,
who forgives all your iniquity,
  who heals all your diseases,
who redeems your life from the Pit,
  who crowns you with steadfast love and mercy
who satisfies you with good as long as you live
  so that your youth is renewed like the eagles.

(103:1-5)

And what if one is bowed low in sorrow and grief? At such times we may be so overwhelmed that words escape us; we cannot find release because we are unable to make our own cry coherent. When this happens we may turn to a psalm such as Psalm 22 with which to express our grief and anguish to God:

My God, my God, why hast thou forsaken me?
  Why art thou so far from helping me, from
    the words of my groaning?
O my God, I cry by day, but thou dost not answer;
  and by night, but find no rest.

(22:1-2)

Even Jesus turned to these very words to carry his anguish to God as he hung from the cross, quoting them in his mother tongue, Aramaic. He knew them so well that they rushed into his mind when his suffering was at full tide. What a tremendous way to express what he was feeling in the darkness of this moment! Many persons are mute in the presence of their deepest emotions. How to put into words what is in their hearts is their greatest need. At such times the Psalms will give voice to their feelings, whether in private or while using the liturgy of the church.

It is obvious that in these psalms the psalmist is speaking

for God. A sense of the reality, power, and goodness of God streams through their words like the sunlight whose shining rays pierce the clouds to touch the earth with glory.

How Were the Psalms First Used?

When we look deeply into the Psalms we discover the Hebrews at worship. In its final form the Psalter became the hymnbook of the second temple. We cannot rightly read and interpret the psalms apart from this realization. Our ritualistic use of them today, while somewhat different from that of the Hebrews, is in line with their practice in the temple services. As Sigmund Mowinckel has shown, there is evidence that some of them were read responsively and also that musical accompaniments were employed although the details are not always clear.[2] Temple singers likewise learned the psalms by heart, even being organized into guilds and families.[3]

Psalms for the Group

Some of the psalms appear to have been written specifically for group worship. Even when the word "I" is used, the reference may be to a corporate body because to the Hebrews the group was more real than the individual. For instance, when the pilgrims went to Jerusalem for the celebration of their feasts, psalms were prepared to be sung as they ascended Mount Zion. The Psalms of Ascents (120-134) are one such collection. Elmer Leslie calls these "Hymns of Pilgrimage."[4] And then there are the Enthronement Psalms (47, 93, 95, 99), which were associated with the enthronement of God as king at the beginning of the new year. Such national celebrations were occasions for group worship of the Lord. The psalms which were written to be used spoke for God as the psalmists in song reminded the nation of its responsibilities and the victories of the Lord.

A moving selection from the Psalms of Ascents is Psalm 121.

As the pilgrim climbs Mount Zion and views the holy hills surrounding Jerusalem he says:

> I lift up my eyes to the hills,
>   From whence does my help come?
> (Vs. 1)

And then the answer follows:

> My help comes from the Lord,
>   who made heaven and earth.
> (Vs. 2)

Because of this conviction that he is in the keeping of the Lord who made the universe he is not afraid to lie down and sleep. God himself will stay awake to watch over him:

> He will not let your foot be moved,
>   he who keeps you will not slumber.
> Behold, he who keeps Israel
>   will neither slumber nor sleep.
> (Vss. 3-4)

Another danger which the pilgrim faced was the possibility of being harmed from the sun or (as they believed) the moon. But he need not fear this because:

> The sun shall not smite you by day,
>   nor the moon by night.
> (Vs. 6)

Through these verses the psalmist suggests God's constant watch-care throughout the entire journey of life, for:

> The Lord will keep
>   your going out and your coming in
>   from this time forth and for evermore.
> (Vs. 8)

Psalms of Great Persons

In addition to the psalms written purposely for group use there were others which express the feelings and thoughts of the individual psalmist and are related to his personal experience. He is as one who is alone as he approaches the Alone; there is a very private issue in the author's life as he presents his problem before God, phrasing it in poetic form. Most great poems are of this kind. Tennyson's "In Memoriam" is a writing in which the author struggles with grief over the death of his friend Arthur Hallam, and moves from doubt to faith. This would be true of most of the great hymns today. They too grew out of an individual's experience.

In spite of the fact that we are persons, separate and different from one another, there are experiences in which we all share. These bind us together so that no man is an island unto himself. It is because of this that one man's poem can become every person's hymn. This is the reason that some of the psalms which were the poems of great souls became used in the worship of the nation Israel as it came to the temple.

It is difficult to say just which of the psalms were primarily individual outpourings of the mood of the soul at the outset, and then were taken up into the worship pattern at the temple because they expressed universal longings and needs. Such confessions as the following are so intimately personal that they may well have had their origin in an individual's experience:

> The Lord is my shepherd, I shall not want;
>   he makes me lie down in green pastures.
> He leads me beside still waters;
>   he restores my soul.
> He leads me in paths of righteousness
>   for his name's sake.
>   (Ps. 23:1-3)
> I sought the Lord, and he answered me.
>   and delivered me from all my fears. . . .

> This poor man cried, and the Lord heard him,
> and saved him out of all his troubles.
>> (Ps. 34:4, 6)
> I waited patiently for the Lord;
> he inclined to me and heard my cry. . . .
> He put a new song in my mouth,
> a song of praise to our God.
>> (Ps. 40:1, 3)
> For I know my transgressions,
> and my sin is ever before me.
> Against thee, thee only, have I sinned,
> and done that which is evil in they sight . . .
>> (Ps. 51:3-4)

The authors of these passages were so centered in God that what they wrote speaks to us of God himself. God had already found them, for he initiated their search for himself.

Who Were the Psalmists?

The authorship of the Psalms is an intriguing question. Traditionally David was regarded as the author of all of them, but this conclusion can hardly be held in view of the content and the headings given to some. Moses is credited with writing Psalm 90, Solomon of Psalms 72 and 127, Ethan the Ezrahite of Psalm 89, and Heman the Ezrahite of Psalm 88. The latter two were probably choirmasters. Even though some of these ascriptions should be questioned, they indicate Israel's belief in multiple authorship.

The internal references to varying backgrounds and conditions also make it highly unlikely that David was their author. In the light of his reputation as a musician and singer of songs, however, the possibility is open that he may have written some of them (I Sam. 18:10). The twenty-third psalm or Shepherd Psalm is one such possibility.

As is true in the case of the narrators and historians of

SAN JOSE BIBLE COLLEGE LIBRARY

Israel, the authors of the Psalms may be regarded as unknown. But their experience of God, revealed in their poems, is widely known as they spoke for God in many and varied situations. Perhaps their anonymity adds to the wonder of what they wrote. Actually, many of the psalms are so revealing that they tell us what the psalmist thinks, longs for, and has experienced, so completely that we feel we know all about him—everything but his name.[5] And God speaks to us through his writing.

When Did the Psalmists Write?

The dates of the several psalms are difficult to establish. If we stress their relationship to similar poetry of the surrounding nations, the tendency is to date them during the period of the monarchy prior to the Exile in Babylon. On the other hand some of them betray post-exilic interests and emphases. But these do not extend as far as the Qumran writings, for the Maccabean accents are absent.

In the history of the interpretation of the Psalms, the pendulum has swung from regarding all of them as pre-exilic to considering them all as post-exilic. The present tendency is to favor a pre-exilic date for most of them.[6] It is the better part of wisdom to keep an open mind in this respect, while at the same time drawing conclusions as seems best in each case.

Historically speaking we are eager to date them with relative exactness. But when this cannot be done, and a loss is felt because we are unable to interpret some of the specific references they contain, there still remains in the Psalms a universal truth, as the psalmists have spoken for God. In a very real sense, religiously speaking, the Psalms belong to all ages, wherever and whenever they are read.

Poetic Form

Our basic assumption all along is that the Psalms are poetic in form. This in itself involves a literary study that takes us afield

22749

from our concern to show that these authors spoke for God. A study of the several literary forms found in the Psalms is involved, yet intriguing. In general it should be said here that the rythm of the original Hebrew in which they were written is not evident in the English translations; this is a distinct loss.

The parallelism or repetition of ideas or their opposites in successive lines, however, can be seen in our translations. There are several types of parallelisms which such a study will spell out and illustrate.[7] The use of stanzas, refrains, strophes, different speaking voices, acrostics, and musical or liturgical directions —all these contribute to the uniqueness of Hebrew poetry as found in the book of Psalms.

A Life Situation Approach

We have already mentioned several types of psalms, those used in connection with the pilgrimages to Jerusalem, and those which celebrated the enthronement of God for the New Year. In this way the Psalms were vitally integrated into the ongoing religious experience of the nation. God speaks through them. They were not collections of poems on a shelf, but a part of the living tissue of the people's life. They were situational and life-centered. The psalmists were speaking for God in terms of actual happenings, attitudes, and longings of the people. We call this the *Sitz im Leben* or life situation approach to interpreting the Psalms, an approach in which they are variously rooted in the cult worship at the temple.

A typical listing of these situations, each calling for a certain literary form, was made by Hermann Gunkel who pioneered in this approach to interpreting the psalms. It includes (1) hymns, (2) laments, both community and individual, (4) enthronement psalms, (5) covenant renewal psalms, (6) psalms of thanksgiving and (7) wisdom or Torah psalms.[8] Others prefer different groupings but in each case there is an astounding indication of the breadth and variety of religious concerns.

I suggest the following classification, which owes much to the work of others, yet includes titles that are to me more definitive: (1) Hymns (Pss. 19, 46, 48, 65, 100, 103, 104, 136); (2) Psalms of individual and community laments (Pss. 6, 22, 38, 51, 123, 130); (3) Songs of confidence and courage (Pss. 23, 27, 62, 91). (4) Psalms of jubliant praise and thanksgiving (Pss. 32, 34, 40, 107, 116); (5) Royal psalms (Pss. 2, 20, 21, 45, 72); (6) Psalms of wisdom (1, 19, 73, 119, 133); (7) Liturgies (Pss. 8, 42, 46); (8) Psalms for pilgrims (Pss. 84, 121, 122), and (9) Enthronement hymns (Pss. 47, 93, 95, 99). Not all the pertinent psalms have been listed under each category; those included, however, are representative. Examples of some of these follow.

A Hymn on the Word of God—Psalm 19

In the religious experience of the Hebrews, God was known in many ways, including his self-revelation in nature (19:1-6) and through the law (19:7-14). Both of these experiences are universal, and therefore Psalm 19, which stresses them, has spoken to men through the centuries since it was written. This was truly something to sing about.

Some scholars regard the praise of nature here as an early writing, while the praise of the law would probably be post-exilic when this emphasis prevailed. But, even so, the marriage of the two into a single psalm is most appropriate for they represent two channels, in no way in opposition to each other, of God's revelation. God speaks in nature; he speaks also in the call to righteous living. Both represent his Word. And in stressing this the psalmist is proclaiming a divine message.

As the psalmist turns to nature he finds here a heavenly language. He is not like the little girl who was first introduced to Tennyson's *Flower in the Crannied Wall,* in which the poet exclaimed that if he could understand the flower in his hand, he would know all about man and God. When her school teacher marveled over this fact, the child shrugged it off and said that she did not find God in flowers because she had learned all about them in botany class. She had heard without *hearing*, and had looked without *seeing*.

In the first part of Psalm 19, however, the author was passing on to others what he had discovered in nature:

> The heavens are telling the glory
> of God;
> and the firmament proclaims his
> handiwork.
>
> (19:1)

He was thrilled with the "silent language" of the sun, and the "quiet knowledge" he found in the nighttime sky.

The law of the Lord was also a source of God's revealing touch. Through it, the psalmist's soul was revived, his confusion dispelled, his heart made happy, and his vision deepened (vss. 7-8). Here is the *summum bonum*; nothing could excel it. Therefore he wants to be certain that his dedication to it is without reserve.

This author's hymn is a dedicatory act, so he closes with a prayer as when sacrifices were offered:

> Let the words of my mouth and the
> meditation of my heart
> be acceptable in thy sight
> O Lord, my rock and my redeemer.
>
> (19:14)

In its entirety this psalm reminds us of the German philosopher Immanuel Kant, who said that the two things that impressed him most were the starry heavens above and the moral law within man.

A Liturgy of Hope—Psalm 42

This psalm tells the story of a pilgrim who longs to go to Jerusalem to celebrate one of the feasts. He has been there before, even leading his friends "in procession to the house of God" (vs. 4). He compares his desire to return to the thirsty search of a young deer for water, and says:

> As a hart longs
>> for flowing streams,
> so longs my soul
>> for thee, O God.
> My soul thirsts for God,
>> for the living God.
> When shall I come and behold
>> the face of God?
>
> (Vss. 1-2)

In spite of this intense desire there are difficulties which he faces and which threaten to interfere with his visit. He may be an exile far to the north, even a prisoner of war. He speaks of the land of the Jordan and of Hermon and Mt. Mizar. Those around him torment him; in derision they ask him, "Where is your God?" (vs. 3). He may have a wound of some sort, or else his soul is injured by the contempt of his enemies (vss. 9-10).

But in spite of all that he has going against him, intermittently in the psalmist's experience there surges up from the depths of his being intimations of faith and hope. He tells himself:

> Why are you cast down, O my soul,
>> and why are you disquieted
>> within me?
> Hope in God; for I shall again praise
>> him,
> my help and my God.
>
> (Vs. 5)

In another one of these glorious moments when faith takes hold, the psalmist says:

> By day the Lord commands his steadfast love;
> and at night his song is with me,
> a prayer to the God of my life.

(Vs. 8)

The psalm closes with a note of full expectation that God will see him through, and the psalmist expresses the same sentiments found in verse 5. His final message to himself and therefore to others is, "Hope in God." This experience of a single individual contained such universal elements of doubt, fear, suffering, and faith that his psalm served others who met at the temple for worship.

A Psalm of Wisdom—Psalm 1

In the following chapter we shall consider the preaching message of the Bible as found in the Wisdom Literature. Psalm 1 is one of the wisdom psalms. In general terms, wisdom writings are of a late date and were intended to spell out the good and righteous way of living. They were grounded in the belief that there was an intelligent structure within life, and the wise man would by experience, examination, and meditation discern, with God's help, this structure and then pursue the path of wisdom.

The psalmist who wrote Psalm 1, was a man of experience; his philosophy of the good way in life reveals years of contemplation and reflection. Like the parable of the Two Foundations (Matt. 7:24-27) in which Jesus compared the wisdom of the wise man who built his house upon the rock with the folly of the foolish man who built his house upon the sand, this psalm compares the wise man who follows the law of the Lord with the foolish man who walks "in the counsel of the wicked,

. . . stands in the way of sinners, . . . and sits in the seat of scoffers" (vs. 1).

In some ways this psalm reminds us also of the Beatitudes of Jesus (Matt. 5:3-12). He begins his poem with the word "blessed." In Hebrew it means, "O how happy. . . !" And it can carry a similar meaning in the Greek which lies behind the Beatitude expression "blessed." In the psalm, however, it is delight in and meditation upon "the law" which makes a man happy, while in the Beatitudes it is in keeping the attitudes of the kingdom that a man finds happiness. The "law" here probably refers not to a written legal code, but to such guidance and instruction as God gives to the man of wisdom.

There is a beauty of literary balance in this psalm, even though it is brief. When it concludes, you feel that the psalmist has made his point and it is time to cease writing; his message is clear:

> For the Lord knows the way of the righteous,
> but the way of the wicked will perish.
> (Vs. 6)

A Liturgy of Victory—Psalm 46

When Martin Luther wrote the hymn "A Mighty Fortress Is Our God" in 1529, he had Psalm 46 in mind. Here is a writing that celebrates the victory of God over his enemies as well as the victory of those who put their faith in him. It is a song of Zion which celebrates the supremacy of the Lord:

> Be still, and know that I am God.
> I am exalted among the nations,
> I am exalted in the earth!
> (Vs. 10)

God's victory, as we have noted, is also the victory of his people, even to the end of the age. The catastrophes which the psalmist mentions—earthquake and flood—are no threat to God. Even though the earth should revert to the chaos out of which it was created (Gen. 1:2), at the end of time the people of God shall not fear, for he is "a very present help in trouble" (vs. 1).

Jerusalem itself will be immovable for:

> God is in the midst of her, she shall
>   not be moved;
> God will help her right early.
>   (Vs. 5)

The nations may rage against her (vs. 6) but to no avail. How beautifully Jerusalem's peacefulness in the face of the storm to come is portrayed!

> There is a river whose streams make
>   glad the city of God,
>   the holy habitation of the Most
>   High.
>   (Vs. 4)

As Elmer Leslie says: "This river represents the quiet, creative, gladdening, saving presence of God, who is present in his Temple on Mount Zion. It stands for the steadying presence of God that will keep Zion from swerving aside in impotent defeat when the world powers of 'darkness grim' are arrayed against her." [9] Because of this the psalm can close with the affirmative message:

> The Lord of hosts is with us;
>   the God of Jacob is our refuge.
>   (Vs. 11)

Modern scholars have increasingly recognized the indebtedness of the psalmists to the poetry of other nations, particularly the Caananites, Assyrians, Babylonians, and Egyptians. They too had their psalms which served a similar function in the life of the people. In their poems, however, the ideas of their own religious outlook predominated, while in those of the Bible, Hebraic ideals, concepts, and experiences were central. A recognition of the fact that religious groups roundabout Israel also had their own psalms is indicative of man's universal search for God and of God's continual outreach toward his children wherever they may be. When the psalmist speaks for God he is bearing witness to the Divine Being who seeks to bring all men to himself.

VII
Wise Men Chart the Way of Wisdom

It has been said with a sense of frustration that the difficulty with life is that it is so daily. Days come and go with dizzying rapidity. How to make them significant is both our longing and our problem. Thomas a Kempis in his *Imitation of Christ* cries out: "O that we had spent but one day in this world thoroughly well." But this is not easily done, for there are obstacles on every hand. Shakespeare put it aptly when he wrote in *As you Like It:* "O, how full of briers is this working-day world!"

The wise men of Israel in their Old Testament writings represented an attempt to provide guidance for meaningful living. As such they were both teachers and preachers. They appealed for disciplined intelligence and moral experience in the lives of persons. Believing that there is a structure within life, it was the better part of wisdom, they urged, to discover it and to adjust one's life accordingly. This has been called "skill in living," requiring judgment that is sound, intelligence, and even shrewdness.

In a recent work, *Wisdom in Israel,* Gerhard von Rad takes the position that this "wisdom" is rooted in man's experiences. These, after reflection, examination, and interpretation led to both new insights and the discovery of principles for living. He sees in Israel, going into the distant past, a constant process of experimentation, and re-examination of these basic guidelines, so that life can be more meaningful.[1] What is the good life? Who is the wise man?

There is yet another and more basic question that should be asked concerning the search of the Hebrews for wisdom. Is asking how to live the good life a godly inquiry? If the answer to this question is affirmative, and it could hardly be otherwise, then we should conclude that the wise men who recorded this body of literature were speaking for God.

Who Were the Wise Men?

The wise men of Israel were preachers in a special category. The enemies of Jeremiah distinguished them from the priests and the prophets when they complained and cried out, "For the law shall not perish from the priest, nor counsel from the wise, nor the word from the prophet" (Jer. 18:18; see also Isa. 29:14). The function of the priest was to preside at the offerings and sacrifices. The prophets spoke forth individually as God called them into his service. They were moved from within by a divine intuition as they spoke for God. With the priests, the flame was on the altar, but with the prophets the flame was in their hearts. In contrast to priests and prophets, the wise men spoke and wrote because they undertook a deliberate and analytical examination of life. The resultant wisdom was believed to come from God. It is interesting to note that the wisdom literature is most prominent in that group of books from the Old Testament known as the *Writings,* as distinguished from the *Law* and the *Prophets.* Like the prophets, the wise men had little to do with institutionalized expressions of religion.

In the study of religion today we are particularly interested in understanding other religious groups. Courses with such titles as "World Religions" and "Religions of Mankind" are quite popular among college youth. In some of these courses, students have an opportunity to study the writings of the wise men of Egypt, Babylon, and Assyria, for they too had their proverbs, fables, riddles, aphorisms, and wisdom addresses.[2] The general term *mashal* is used to cover several types of such writings. The discovery of this broad "international" base for wisdom writings among other religions is a witness to God's universal revelation, in addition to his particular Word in the Hebrew tradition which has its own special accents and status.[3]

All along we have been emphasizing the great variety of personal types who were called to speak for God. The same is true among the writers of wisdom. Some of them were craftsmen and artists; some were counselors to kings; others were promoters of the occult—magicians, sorcerers, astrologers, and diviners (Isa. 3:2-3). And among them also were women (II Sam. 20:14-22).

The leading literary works of the men of wisdom in the Old . Testament include Proverbs, Job, and Ecclesiastes. In addition to these there are such psalms as 1, 19, 73, 119, and 133.[4] Even the Apocrypha contains similar writings in such books as Ecclesiasticus, the Wisdom of Solomon, Tobit, I Esdras, and Baruch.

Proverbs—New and Old

Have you ever heard the old saw or adage "A stitch in time saves nine"? Perhaps you are familiar with, "A watched pot never boils," or "They don't know it now, but they are eating their white bread." These are proverbs which have come down to us from the past. They represent wisdom distilled from experience. In our own day at least two statements spoken in crisis hours so completely gathered together the thinking and emotions of the people that they have become proverbial. President Franklin D. Roosevelt in the midst of the depression said publicly: "The greatest thing we have to fear is fear itself." And President John F. Kennedy in his inaugural address said: "Ask not what your country can do for you but what you can do for your country." This is how proverbs are born today as well as how they arose in the distant past.

How is it that we can say that God spoke through the proverbs of the Hebrew people? It was not because these statements were cleverly phrased, or that they were easily recalled. Rather, it was because they were rooted and confirmed in experience, and this means that they were grounded in the nature of the universe—in God. They were true to life and represented God's ordering of nature and human existence.

It is difficult to identify the authors of the maxims in the book of Proverbs. Most of them were attributed to Solomon because of his prayer for wisdom when he became king. After referring to the greatness of his father, David, he said: "Thou hast made thy servant king in place of David my father, although I am but a little child; I do not know how to go out or come in. . . . Give thy servant therefore an understanding mind to govern thy people, that I may discern between good and evil . . ." (I Kings 3:7, 9). His petition was granted, and the king achieved a reputation for wisdom far and wide. He was even visited by the queen of Sheba, who had heard of his wisdom and who, after seeing him, exclaimed: "The half was not told to me; your wisdom and prosperity surpass the report which I heard" (I Kings 10: 1-10). Stories such as the one about the two women who each claimed the same infant as her own and how Solomon picked the true mother were circulated about the king (I Kings 3:16-22).

Because of Solomon's reputation for wisdom great numbers of the proverbs were attributed to him, although others were assigned to Agur (Prov. 30) and Lemuel (Prov. 31). It is not likely that he authored many of these, for they represent a collection covering many decades. The book of Proverbs is a deposit of the wisdom of the Hebrew people through successive generations. It may be, however, that at Solomon's court the "wisdom" of the Orient was first introduced. Probably this led, in turn, to a training program for youth of high standing as they prepared to take significant positions in the society of the day. The proverbs would make up the curriculum that was used.

Put God First

Because the proverbs were concerned for a practical way of life, based upon reflection on experience and philosophical judgment, they did not relegate God to a secondary place. Listen to the wise man who writes:

> Trust in the Lord with all your
> heart,

> and do not rely on your own
>   insight.
> In all your ways acknowledge him,
>   and he will make straight your
>   paths.
>
> (Prov. 3:5-6)

In true wisdom form the wise man is concerned to find a right "path" for daily living. The important note here is that he advocates trust in God as the true source of wisdom.

Be Not Lazy

One of the hazards to personal development and social contribution is laziness. Like Jesus, who chastized the foolish maidens who had neglected the business of putting oil in their lamps (Matt. 25:1-13). the wise man warned the youth in his day against being sluggardly. He wrote:

> Go to the ant, O sluggard;
>   consider her ways, and be wise.
> Without having any chief,
>   officer or ruler,
> she prepares her food in summer,
>   and gathers her sustenance in
>   harvest. . . .
> A little sleep, a little slumber,
>   a little folding of the hands to
>   rest,
> and poverty will come upon you like a
>   vagabond,
>   and want like an armed man.
>
> (Prov. 6:6-8, 10-11)

In reading these words we are reminded of the statement in the Gospel of John where Jesus says: "My Father is working still, and I am working" (5:17). Creation continues for God; should not man keep active too?

Avoid Angry Words

The universal temptation to utter angry words when tempers run hot was also real to the wise men of the past. One of them wrote:

> A soft answer turns away wrath,
>   but a harsh word stirs up anger.
> The tongue of the wise despenses knowledge,
>   but the mouths of fools pour out folly. . . .
> A gentle tongue is a tree of life,
>   but perverseness in it breaks the
>   spirit.
>
> (Prov. 15:1-2, 4)

One cannot but wonder to what extent Jesus might have pondered these words of the wise man. Could they possibly have been in his mind when he urged turning the other cheek, and returning good for evil (Matt. 5:39)?

Look to Your Heart

The psalms of Israel often express in poetry the teachings of the prophets. The same is true of the wisdom literature; prophetic emphases frequently can be seen in the proverbial forms of the wise men. Note that in the following there is a reflection of the prophet's words against ritualistic substitutes for justice:

> Every way of a man is right in his
>   own eyes,
>   but the Lord weighs the heart.
> To do righteousness and justice
>   is more acceptable to the Lord
>   than sacrifice.
>
> (Prov. 21:2-3)

How like the words of the prophet Hosea when he said for God: "I desire steadfast love and not sacrifice" (6:6)! Again this proverb sounds like Amos who cried: "I hate, I despise your feasts. . . . But let justice roll down like waters, and righteousness like an everflowing stream" (5:21, 24).

Keep Wisdom and Knowledge

Book III (22:17–24:22) of Proverbs is best understood as based upon the Egyptian Book of Wisdom, *The Instruction of Amen-em-Opet,* which contained instructions of a teacher as he guided young men into the good life (see note 5). It begins with an introduction that sets forth the purpose of the proverbs and urges dedicated study of them:[5]

> Incline your ear, and hear the words
> of the wise,
> and apply your mind to my
> knowledge; . . .
> That your trust may be in the Lord,
> I have made them known to you
> today, even to you. . . .
> to show you what is right and true,
> that you may give a true answer
> to those who sent you?
> (Prov. 22:17-21)

The goals of wisdom are spelled out here; they include trusting the Lord so that one may be shown what is right and true. The student who is seeking such knowledge must listen, hear, and apply his mind. Note that the intellectual aspect of the wise man's life as he listens to his teacher is stressed.

The Book of Job
Faith in God and Human Suffering

Human suffering has long plagued both the body and the mind. It has to be physically felt and endured; it drives us to reflection and philosophy. It also becomes a theological issue when faced in the light of the character of God as one who is loving, righteous, and powerful.

Some have attempted to deny its reality through positive affirmations. Others have borne it stoically without asking ultimate questions. Still others are led to denying the existence of God in the face of suffering; an attempt to hold on to one's faith at such times is painful to them. And then there are those who stress the fruits of suffering, convinced that it leads to an enrichment of character and a deepening understanding of both God and man.

Leo Tolstoy the great Russian novelist believed that it was by those who suffered that the world has been advanced. In World War I, Cardinal Mercier saw his home torn by shells, the cathedral he loved leveled to a pile of debris, his valuable library burned and some of his students killed. Surely there was enough here to depress and confound him. But after the holocaust had ended, he said: "Suffering accepted and vanquished . . . will give you a serenity which may well prove the most exquisite fruit of your life." [6]

The American novelist and playwright Thornton Wilder has concerned himself with suffering in such novels as *The Bridge of San Luis Rey,* and the plays *Our Town* and *The Skin of Our Teeth.* He also wrote a series of three-minute plays in which suffering was sometimes the theme. In one of these, *The Angel That Troubled the Waters,* he pictured a doctor who was ill, standing at the side of the pool of Bethesda. When the waters were about to be "troubled" (John 5:2-9), and he was on the verge of entering, the angel said to him: "Stand back. Healing is not for you. Without your wound where would your power be that sends your low voice trembling into the hearts of men. . . . In love's service only wounded soldiers will do." [7]

There is wisdom in these statements by Tolstoy, Mercier, and Wilder. Each emphasizes the fact that suffering disciplines and deepens life. The wisdom literature of the Hebrews also was concerned with suffering, both as a fact of life and in the way man carried his pain. This is particularly true in the Book of Job. In its own special manner, instead of quoting maxims from the past as in Proverbs, it presents a dramatic discussion of the faith-problem in the life of the righteous man who suffers. The issue of the suffering of a good person is also to be found in Babylonian and Sumerian sources, but the biblical account of Job has its own Hebraic character and solution to the problem.

The heart of the Book of Job (3:1–42:6) is a lengthy dialogue in poetical form between Job and his three friends on the one hand, and between Job and God on the other. Preceding (1:1–2:13) and following (42:7-17) this extended poem is an ancient folktale which is used to set the stage for the dialogue. The folktale may date back to the second millennium B.C. in oral form and 1,000 to 600 B.C. in written form, whereas the poetical section may be dated somewhere between the sixth and third centuries.

Why did the unknown author of the poem at the heart of the book of Job write this most outstanding of all literary works in the field of suffering? Was he speaking for himself or for God? Could he have personally been caught in the agonized backwash of the Exile, a staggering event that also brought forth such depths of understanding as found in II Isaiah (40-55)? Surely this was not simply an academic discussion that he was writing, for it plunges to the depths of the issue with agonizing cries of despair and concern.

Plagued by the supercilious platitudes of his three friends who argue with him, implying that he must be guilty of sin or he would not have suffered such losses of wealth and family or have experienced such personal pain, Job continually holds on to his own conscience. He had done nothing to deserve this tragedy, hence he cried out:

> Oh, that I knew where I might find
> him [God],

> that I might come even to his seat!
> I would lay my case before him
> and fill my mouth with arguments.
> I would learn what he would answer
> me,
> and understand what he would
> say to me.
> Would he contend with me in the
> greatness of his power?
> No; he would give heed to me.
> There an upright man could reason
> with him,
> and I should be acquitted for ever
> by my judge.
>
> (23:3-7)

How long can a man remain in continued agony? Still he turns to God as he says:

> God has cast me into the mire,
> and I have become like dust and
> ashes.
> I cry to thee and thou dost not answer
> me;
> I stand, and thou dost not heed me.
>
> (30:19-20)

Where is the answer to be found? Is there an answer? Surely Job's continual affirmations of his own worth are getting him nowhere. There must be another road to truth. At this point in the poem, Job is taken on an intellectual tour of the universe where he is dumbfounded and speechless in the presence of the greatness and power of God. Hugh Anderson describes Job's state of soul and says: "Before this God Job is silenced; he has not one plea or claim left; he has no longer any merit of his own. He has found the God *who is God,* who is higher than all human reckoning, who can only be adored, and in whose presence man is fit only to repent in dust and ashes." [8] Finally Job bows his head and heart before God and says:

I know that thou canst do all
    things,
and that no purpose of thine can
    be thwarted.
Therefore I have uttered what I did
    not understand,
    things too wonderful for me, which
    I did not know.
I had heard of thee by the hearing of
    the ear,
    but now my eye sees thee;
therefore I despise myself,
    and repent in dust and ashes.
                (42:2-6)

Through these words of Job in the writing of the unknown author, God has spoken to man for more than twenty-five centuries. This comes near to being salvation by faith as the New Testament knows it, except that in the latter it is the redeeming Christ who is the reason for high belief.[9]

Ecclesiastes

The Words of the Preacher

R. B. Y. Scott opens his commentary on Ecclesiastes with the statement: "Ecclesiastes is the strangest book in the Bible, or at any rate the book whose presence in the sacred canons of Judaism and of Christianity is most inexplicable." [10] A close examination of this third-century B.C. work which stresses the futility of life in its constant repetitions of seasons and experiences, and comes to the conclusion, which it affirms at the outset, that "All is vanity" (1:2), would seem to confirm this judgment.

Passage after passage is out of step with the burning faith of the prophets and the victorious stance which Job ultimately reached: "I have seen everything that is done under the sun; and behold, all is vanity and a striving after wind" (Eccles. 1:

14). Yes, he believed, after applying his mind to seek and search out by wisdom all that is done under the heavens, that "it is an unhappy business that God has given to the sons of men to be busy with" (1:13).

The "preacher" does not deny the existence of God, but finds him unknowable and his ways beyond comprehension. As in the Greek view of history, all things are constantly on the move, the cycle is repeated over and over but nothing gets anywhere; there is no real change. In spite of man's character, his fate is as the fate of beasts.

What shall man do in such a universe? What is the way of wisdom? In a word it is to enjoy what is given us day by day, and to expect nothing in the end but oblivion. This is the philosophy of resignation, and although it is pessimistic, it is based upon reflection.

The selection of this writing as a part of scripture probably was due to its assignment to Solomon as the author (1:1). The earliest Christian commentator on the book was Gregory Thaumaturgus, who said that its purpose was "to show that all the affairs and pursuits of men are vain and useless, in order to lead us to the contemplation of heavenly things." In other words, the books speaks for God indirectly, in that it impels us to accept the vanity of earthly life as a prod to seek for God.

Another unknown seeker after wisdom who admired the reflections of the "preacher," but feared that they might confuse others or mislead them attached a postscript to the book (12:9-14). In it he urged that men may say many things, for "of making many books there is no end." He even implies that it is possible to do too much thinking about life. What wise men have written may be only "goads" to understanding. And then he counsels: "Fear God, and keep his commandments; for this is the whole duty of man. For God will bring every deed into judgment, with every secret thing, whether good or evil" (vss. 13-14). Men must live responsibly before God, for there is a final word to life and it is God who speaks it.

VIII
Gospel Writers Announce Good News

The usual answer of the uninformed to the question as to what a gospel is would probably be that it is a life of Jesus. Judged by our understanding of biography today this answer would be incorrect. What we have come to associate with a biography includes a consideration of background, boyhood, youth, et cetera. Our Gospels do not contain any of these except for Luke's brief account of Jesus' visit to Jerusalem at the age of twelve (2:41-51). When we meet Jesus in any significant way in these records he is already a young adult who comes to John the Baptist's revival requesting baptism.

And the story of Jesus' ministry which follows in the Gospels is not in the accepted form of a biography. There are gaps in the record. What is included is highly selective, and the several miracle stories, sermonic utterances, teachings, and community contacts are presented sporadically and without continuity. The Gospel of Mark provides the outline for both Matthew and Luke, although each adds individual materials, while the Gospel of John goes its own chronological way in line with its purpose and goal.

A Gospel is an account of the ministry and message of Jesus in which bits of narrative, selected sayings, and the Christian community understandings are put together in various ways in order to inform, meet opposition, settle controversy, and win converts. A special approach to analyzing these materials from a literary standpoint is referred to today as *form criticism*. Its chief proponents include such scholars as Bultmann, Dibelius, Schmidt, Taylor, Scott, Redlich, Grant, and Koch.

In this study a variety of names are given to the several literary forms that are found in the Gospels. For instance, E. F. Scott in *The Validity of the Gospel Record* (p. 119) listed miracle stories, paradigms or pronouncement stories, aphorisms, tales, legends, controversies, and apocalyptic utterances. Different scholars select other titles and arrangements, but the principle of the use of various literary forms by the Gospel writers is basic in each case.

Some writers find more historical validity than others in these several forms, usually depending upon their conclusions regarding the place of the Christian community in gathering, preserving, or tooling them to fit specific purposes. It has been a productive approach and has been helpful in our understanding not only of what a Gospel is, but also of the motive behind its being written and the character of the material that goes into its making as well as its nature and construction.[1]

The Gospel Writers as Preachers

Why did a Gospel writer produce a Gospel? Was it not mainly because he had a message to proclaim? And in this sense was he not a preacher who spoke for God? As such does he not take his place among the others in the Old and New Testaments who proclaimed the Word?

In his Foreword to *Sermons Preached in a University Church,* George A. Buttrick writes: "This is a book of sermons. . . . Preaching is specific: its language is particular, and it is addressed to a particular congregation. The diction of the preacher is that of the historian and dramatist, not that of the philosopher, for preaching appeals *by* the history-drama of the Event of Christ *to* the willed drama of men's daily history."[2] This is exactly what the authors of the Gospels were doing. Something had happened—an Event—which had changed their own lives, and the lives of others. It should be shared with still others so that they too could respond. The fact that they were not sharing it vocally becomes pedantic. Their writing constituted an act of preaching. They were delivering a message.

By way of history it is suggestive here to recall that Papias (*ca.* 60-130), who was the bishop of Hierapolis in Asia Minor, is reported in Eusebius' *Ecclesiastical History* as saying that the

Gospel of Mark rested upon John Mark's memory as the interpreter of the message of Peter.[3] Surely this is not all that we have in the Gospel of Mark, and the statement raises a number of questions, but it does open the way for the conclusion that some Christian preaching underlies the First Gospel.

The preaching element in the New Testament has received considerable attention during recent decades. This interest was aroused particularly by C. H. Dodd in *The Apostolic Preaching and Its Development.* Here Dodd presented a critical analysis of early Christian preaching. He made a distinction between the *kerygma,* which is the preaching message of the church, and the *didache,* which is its ethical instruction.

It is my view here that the unity of the New Testament is to be found in this preaching message which centered in the Lord Jesus, "(1) whose origin was in God, (2) who was the agent of creation, (3) whose advent was prophesied, (4) who came in the flesh, (5) who as the Messiah proclaimed the Kingdom and performed mighty works, (6) who died for man's sin according to the Scriptures, (7) who was raised from the dead, (8) who ascended in glory to God's right hand, (9) who was present in the spirit as living Lord to bring newness of life to his followers, (10) who established, indwelt, and guided the church, (11) who would return at the end of the Age to judge, bless, and overcome all evil in men, nations, and the spirit world, and (12) who ultimately would reign with God in an eternal kingdom." [4]

The Gospel writers participate in announcing this preaching message along with the rest of the biblical authors. They, no doubt, were addressing in their own way the same Christian community to whom the other writers spoke. They too were preachers because they had a kerygma or preaching message.

The introduction to the Gospel of Luke (1:1-4) presents in capsule form an illustration of this point of view. The author says that even though others had written of the events which centered in Jesus, he too wanted to tell his story of these things.

He had been giving careful thought to them for some time, speaking to eyewitnesses, sifting out the data and arranging it into some orderly sequence, while making sure of its validity. All of this was in order that Theophilus, who had already received some instruction along these lines, might know the truth of these matters. He wanted to convert Theophilus, not simply to inform him.

Addressing a Cause

We err when we think of the Gospels solely as chronicles of what Jesus said and did. They contain a record of his words and deeds, to be sure, but they are more like weapons fashioned to serve in a mighty cause than reference works. Great events were taking place both within and without the Christian community calling for thought and action. And the Gospel writers proclaimed the needed message for these situations. They spoke for God in the midst of living issues; this accounts for their vitality as written documents.

Mark Speaks to a Cause

Take the Gospel of Mark. It may be regarded as having been written in Rome not long after the persecutions by Nero. Controversy, rejection, and even martyrdom were the threat of the hour. Paul and Peter had recently been killed because of their position as Christians.[5] The Christian community needed an instrument to bring strength, and this the Gospel provided. Mark emphasizes Jesus' message that to follow him one must be willing to pay a price (8:34-38; 9:35; 10:29-31, 35-45). He was probably the companion of Peter, nephew of Barnabas, and traveling companion of Paul on his first missionary journey.[6]

The church was also in need of shedding its Jewish character as it was finding a place in the gentile world. Gentile Christians must discover in Jesus a broader outlook than a traditional Judaistic interpretation of his message provided, and this Mark gave to them (2:26; 6:14, 17; 7:1-8, 14-23, 31; 8:10; 14:12). This meant lifting up certain sayings of Jesus as well as particular references to his activities in the tradition and setting them forth as a specific for what was needed. Is not this what all preachers are continually called upon to do if their message is to be relevant?

Matthew Speaks to a Cause

At the time when the Gospel of Matthew was written there was need for extended missionary activity. During the last quarter of the first century (ca. A.D. 85) this called for a definition of the faith in the face of Jewish opposition. Arguments against Christianity in the Jewish synagogues throughout the Greco-Roman world were vigorous and constant, and an equally vigorous reply was necessary. It has been suggested that Matthew was written as though there were a Jewish synagogue just across the street where the author could constantly hear what was being said. And in his Gospel he makes reply.

Here again Matthew, like Mark, arranged and presented the gospel tradition so as to meet the actual needs of the times.[7] The Great Commission called for continued church expansion (28:18-20), as did the promise that "gospel of the kingdom will be preached throughout the whole world, as a testimony to all nations" before the end of the age (24:14), the latter a matter of great concern to Matthew. Particularly important in this situation were the words of Jesus concerning his purpose to fulfill the law rather than to destroy it (5:17-48). Jesus also offered guidance for daily living, as did the law (6:1–7:27). Matthew was eager to show that Jesus' life, death, and ministry fulfilled Jewish prophecy. He cited more than one hundred and thirty Old Testament passages in his Gospel; some are spoken by Jesus himself and others are the author's own selections in order to explain what Jesus said and did.

We find here a deliberate attempt on the part of the author to drive home his points through the medium of a Gospel.[8] He was selective in his use of sources and arrangement of material, alternating teaching sections with narrative accounts. It is possible that he even divided his Gospel into five sections in order to parallel the five books of the law.[9] This would impress Jewish readers. He has a cause to represent, a need to meet, and a message to announce. He speaks for God in his own day and age, and continues to do so in ours.

Luke Speaks to a Cause

We have already noted Luke's preface in which he described both his purpose and process in writing his Gospel. It indicated a sense of responsibility in discovering and presenting the truth, something about his working habits, and a final statement concerning his goal. We cannot claim for Luke the procedures of a technical modern historian, for he did not have our tools in hand. But there was in his approach to the task a breadth and depth that present-day writers and preachers can emulate.

John Henry Jowett was a prince among preachers, both in England and the United States. His Lyman Beecher lectures on preaching should be read at least once a year by today's preachers. His advice concerning the need for breadth of approach in sermon preparation reminds me of Luke's preface. Jowett says: "We must be explorers of a vast continent of truth, and the individual texts will find us out as we go along. . . . Men whose eyes range over the vast prairies have intense discernment of things that are near at hand." [10]

Such an outlook as Jowett's accounts in part for Luke's large inclusion of special materials (9:51–18:14), his broad humanitarian interest, and his concern for details in writing a narrative. His breadth of interest in the events surrounding the ministry of Jesus led him to follow the writing of his Gospel with the writing of the book of Acts in which he describes the experiences of the early church, the beginning of world missions, and the arrival of Paul in Rome, the center of the empire.

The Third Gospel has been assigned to several places of origin: Ephesus, Corinth, and Rome—since each was in the heart of the Greco-Roman world where the causes that were of concern to the author were present. The identity of the author is also disputed, although he most likely was the beloved physician who accompanied Paul on some of his missionary travels, and whom the apostle mentions several times in his letters.[11]

As a preacher, Luke was writing in order to meet certain issues that were threatening the church in his own day (ca. A.D. 85-90). He could have done so by writing an essay or a set of epistles, to be sure, but like the other evangelists he chose a gospel form instead. By presenting the story of Jesus in a way that highlighted certain attitudes and teachings of his Lord, he not only would get his point across but do it in a way that gave it the authority of Jesus himself. And at the same time he would be writing a Gospel which proclaimed the good news. A Gospel is a unique literary form that the church probably invented, since we do not find Gospels before the Christian movement.

WERE THE CHRISTIANS LOYAL TO THE STATE?

One of the major issues confronting the church at this time was its relation to the state. Rome had recognized various religions. They were permitted (religio lecita); Judaism was one of these, and as long as Christianity was regarded as a Jewish sect it was accepted. But by this time, both because of its teachings and its persecution at the hands of the Jews, it was being pushed outside the "permitted" circle. The fact also that Jesus had been crucified by the state as a political criminal placed the church under suspicion.

If only the Romans, ruled by Domitian (A.D. 81-96), who distrusted and later persecuted the Christians, had read Luke's record of Pilate's statement as the Roman procurator when Jesus was brought before him for trial: "I find no crime in this man" (Luke 23:4), had taken note of the fact that King Herod refused to pass judgment upon him (23:6-12), had listened to the Roman centurion declare at the crucifixion: "Certainly this man was innocent" (23:47)—if only these men's actions had been regarded seriously by the Roman officials, it would have been clear that Jesus and his followers were not revolutionaries seeking to overthrow the Roman state. This had been Luke's hope and a part of his preaching message as he spoke for God.

But there is more. In Luke it is stressed that the Christians were loyal to the Jewish temple, and even charged by Jesus to make the usual offering for cleansing (5:14; 17:14). Jesus also taught in its precincts during the final week of his life (21: 37). He commended a Roman soldier for his faith (7:1-10), called a collector of Roman taxes to be a disciple, and fraternized with others (5:27-32; 15:1; 19:1-10). He even advocated paying taxes to Caesar for the services the state had rendered (20:21-25).

The relation between the church and the state is not a peripheral issue. We have seen in this century the dire results of totalitarianism. When six million Jews can be put to death by the state in gas furnaces, and a Dietrich Bonhoeffer executed for treason, we can see that this is not a past issue. In all these biblical situations Luke presents Jesus as not antistate *per se;* he is not an anarchist, for he appreciates the function of the state under God. *Yet men must first of all give to God what is God's* (Luke 20:25).[12]

LUKE'S UNIVERSALISM

There is a breadth in Luke's presentation that is so specific and evident that we may conclude that this too was a part of his preaching message. Just as Matthew stresses Jewish relationships, so Luke emphasizes God's love for outcasts and gentiles.

Not only the lost sheep of Israel were to hear the gospel, but God's children everywhere were to receive the good news (Luke 9:1-6; 10:1-12).

It was a common belief in that day that there were seventy nations in the world. In Luke's inclusion of Jesus' sending out the seventy (10:1-12), a narrative which he alone presents, we can see this evangelist proclaiming the universality of God's salvation in Christ. And in his special notation of the place Jesus made for women in the kingdom, we can see another illustration of Luke's emphasis upon the fact that the gospel was for all humanity (8:2-3; 23:27-31, 49; 24:10-11). How relevant this is as we work for the inclusive society today!

John Speaks to a Cause

Halford Luccock once wrote that: "The gospel was not merely an idea, a message, but an idea *in process of communication. . . . When it loses that motion of communication, it ceases to be itself.*" [13] The authors of the Gospels were preaching, communicating the gospel in every line they wrote. They had no other purpose in mind and would have agreed with Henry Sloane Coffin's emendation of Phillips Brooks' definition of preaching as "truth through personality" so that it read "*truth through personality to a person.*"

This is startlingly evident in John's explanation of his reason for writing when he said: "These are written that you may believe that Jesus is the Christ, the Son of God, and that believing you may have life in his name" (20:31). John had something to say to persons because he believed that Jesus Christ had something to say—and do—to them.

THE RETURN OF CHRIST

The persons to whom John was speaking for God as he wrote his Gospel were caught up in a situation so involved that it constituted a cause. Some were disillusioned because the promised return of Christ had not occurred, and the overthrow of the emperor had not happened as they had anticipated it would. The book of Revelation had been written about A.D. 96. It was already A.D. 100-110 at this time, and its prophecies seemed not to have been fulfilled.[14] Why not? When would they be?

John gave them a spiritual gospel, nonapocalyptic in character, in which he stressed the fact that the return of Jesus in the Spirit to indwell men's hearts had already occurred (John 14: 16-18). Even God's judgment promised in the Apocalypse of John was taking place constantly as men chose darkness rather than the light (3:17-18; 9:39-40).

CONFLICTS WITH THE GREEKS

There were yet other issues to be faced. The early Christians, particularly those who lived abroad, were surrounded by Greek thought, which challenged the point of view of the church. And this provided causes that must be met. For instance, John stressed Jesus' teaching on the new birth to meet the claims of the Greek mystery religions that this was already provided through their initiations. But the true new birth, which brought eternal life, came through belief in Christ (John 1:12-13; 3:1 ff; 4:1-42).

Then there were the Docetists among the Gnostics who attacked the reality of Jesus' fleshly life. Was not this the reason John in the Prologue stressed that the Word had become *actual flesh* (1:14)? The Gnostics also emphasized the creative act of the Logos or divine reason. Would not John's presentation of Jesus as the true Logos or Word challenge this teaching (1:1-3)? It was through him that "all things were made" (1:3).

CONFLICTS WITH THE JEWS

The challenge which the arguments of the Jews in the Greco-Roman world against Jesus presented to the Christians are particularly reflected in John's account of the confrontation with them when Jesus attended the Feast of Tabernacles (John 7–8). He appears to be talking to Jews in his own day, and no doubt he did so, *but we also find here reflected the objections of the Jews in a later period to Christian claims about Jesus.* And John is answering them by giving Jesus' replies. He is speaking for God in assembling these remarks in his Gospel.

The Jews objected because Jesus was unschooled. The answer given is that Jesus' teaching came from God and anyone who wills to do his will shall be convinced of this truth (John 7:14-17). Jesus' breaking of the Sabbath law, which implied his loose handling of all Jewish Law, was next criticized by the Jews. The reply is that they broke it also, as in the case of circumcision on the Sabbath (7:18-24).

Again, the Jews found fault with Jesus' known origin; the coming of the Messiah was to be mysterious. Jesus then tells them that his origin in reality is in God (John 7:27-29). Then the Jews turned to a remark Jesus made that he was going away, which they interpreted to mean that he was to become a turncoat and go to the Greeks abroad. No, said Jesus, I am returning to God and "Where I am you cannot come" (7:33-36).

These issues above illustrate how the Fourth Gospel is a situational writing, prepared in gospel form to meet problems in the church. Like the synoptic writers, the author, who was probably a pupil of the apostle John the witness (John 19:35), was proclaiming a message in his own day; he was preaching to meet actual needs of the church in the Greek world.[15] Like Mark Matthew, and Luke, he does his job in his own way, using the tradition he has inherited, including probably the Synoptic Gospels and recording also what the living Christ, speaking through the Spirit, was directing him to set down.

The Gospel Portrait of Jesus

We have been examining certain "causes" which the Gospels sought to meet. This helps us to see them as writings which constitute the sword of the Lord, doing battle for righteousness. A living church was speaking to itself and meeting its own needs, as well as addressing the outside world. And it was using the gospel form which placed Jesus in the center of the picture as Christ the Lord. Their dynamic character was rooted in the integrity of their purpose. They were not dead records of a dead past, but bore a living witness to what had happened in their own day—and was still happening. There God's word was personalized in the deeds and message of the Son.

We are fortunate in having four Gospels in that each presents its portrait of Jesus from its own perspective. The word *portrait* is chosen deliberately because the representation of Jesus that is given us is more than a photographic image. It includes interpretation as well as pictorialization. We should not feel the need to put ourselves in the position of having to make a selection among the four. Each carries its own truth in the portrait it presents. It takes all four to complete the portrayal of the whole person of Jesus—what he was like, what he did, what he said, who he was, and what his life and death meant for his own day—and mean throughout all time.

In a very real sense we can say that the Gospel writers were preaching Jesus. They were offering him to their readers as the living Lord with the hope that there would be a response. They cared about the outcome even as an evangelist who preaches in a revival. It is interesting in this connection that the title sometimes given to the writers of the Gospels is "the Four Evangelists."

Jesus is portrayed in the Gospel of Mark as the Messiah who is the Son of God (1:1). He overcomes the kingdom of demons so that the people comment: "With authority he commands even the unclean spirits and they obey him" (1:27b). He is the activist who in dynamic fashion undertakes the work of the Promised One in Israel.

The Gospel of Matthew emphasized Jesus as the descendant

of David and traces his lineage back to Abraham (1:1). He fulfills Old Testament prophecy (2:5-6; 2:15, etc.) even though he sometimes sets himself above the law when he says "But I say to you" (5:22, 28, 32, 34, 39, 44). He is the New Moses, the church is the New Israel, and the Lord's Supper institutes the New Covenant in his blood. Jesus is seen as Lord over the New Age which is now come upon them and is yet to come in its fullness at the end of time (24:3-5, 29-30).

In the Gospel of Luke we see Jesus as the Lord of all humanity. Even in the genealogy Luke carries the line back to "Adam, the Son of God" (3:38). He cares for Jews and Gentiles alike (10:33 ff; 14:15 ff), and is concerned for outcasts and sinners who were too often pushed aside by the respectable religious leaders (5:30-32; 7:36 ff; 15:1). Luke alone of all the Gospels calls Jesus "Savior" (2:11). He also alone tells us that on the cross Jesus prayed for his enemies (23:34), forgave the repentant and dying thief (23:43), and committed his spirit to God as he died (23:46). And Luke's unique resurrection narrative of the risen Christ's walk to Emmaus is the fullest and in some ways the richest of all the accounts of this event (24:13 ff). Throughout Luke's Gospel, Jesus is represented as a man of prayer who not only taught men to pray (11:1-2, 5-8; 18:1-8, 9-14), but also prayed himself, daily and at the crisis hours of his life (3:21; 5:16; 6:12; 9:16; 29 ff; 10:21-22; 11:1; 22:31-32; 22:41, 44; 23:46).

The Gospel of John presents its portrait of Jesus in exalted terms. His origin as the Logos or Word is within the very being of God (1:1), and he is the agent of creation itself (1:3). From first to last, in John, Jesus is the Christ, the Son of God who gives life to those who believe in him (20:31). The author sees him as one who performed "signs," seven miracles which constituted a complete witness and indicated his nature and how he gave life for men (2:1 ff; 4:46 ff; 5:1 ff; 6:1 ff; 6:16 ff; 9:1 ff; 11:1 ff).

The person of Christ is presented by John as the basic necessity for life itself as humans must live it. He is "the bread of life" (6:35), "the light of the world" (8:12), "the door of the sheep" (10:7), "the good shepherd" (10:14), "the resurrection and the life" (11:25), "the way, and the truth and the life" (14:6) and "the true vine" (15:1). Without any of these, true existence would cease.

The portraits of Jesus in the Four Gospels constitute a preaching message. They are the good news which the authors proclaim. They are offering to those who read the "bread of life" and the "light of the world." The Gospels are far more than a telling of the story of Jesus; they constitute a plea to respond to Jesus. This is preaching, no less.

In commenting on "the bread of life" which Jesus offers, Bultmann points to man's universal hunger for life that does not perish and adds: "If man wants eternal life, he must find the food which endures." This is what Jesus offers, and this is what John the evangelist urges men to eat.[16]

IX
Jesus Came Preaching

What is it that makes a preacher a *preacher* rather than a teacher? Is it what he says or the way in which he says it? Do preaching and teaching sometimes overlap?

Preacher—Teacher

Jesus was referred to as a preacher from the outset of his ministry. Mark reported that after the arrest of John the Baptist, "Jesus came into Galilee, *preaching* the gospel of *God*" (1:14).[1] He is also spoken of as a preacher by Mark when the evangelist notes that Jesus felt he must leave Capernaum and visit other towns, "that I may *preach* there also" (1:38); Mark then states that he "went throughout all Galilee, *preaching* in their synagogues and casting out demons" (1:39). Matthew (4:17, 23; 9:35; 11:1), and Luke (4:44; 8:1) also refer to Jesus as a preacher.

Jesus is sometimes spoken of as a teacher (Mark 5:35: Matt. 12:38; Luke 18:18). Martha tells her sister, Mary, in the Gospel of John that: "The *Teacher* is here and is calling for you" (11:28). In this Gospel he is also called *Rabbi,* which means teacher, when two followers of John the Baptist inquire where he is staying (1:38). And at the tomb the tearful Mary cries out to the risen Lord "*Rabboni*" (20:16), a title which likewise means teacher.

There is some overlapping in the use of the words preacher and teacher in the Gospels. Both appear to be employed interchangeably when referring to the same type of activity. Even today a good preacher will also be teaching as he delivers his sermon, and a responsible teacher may sometimes be preaching when he is personally moved by the truth he is enunciating. When one shares truth and enthusiastically and sincerely recommends it at the same time, is he not assuming somewhat the role of a preacher? This point could possibly be argued, but the line between teaching and preaching sometimes becomes quite thin. In Jesus' case there were occasions when there was no line of separation at all between the two.[2]

The Effect of Jesus' Preaching

We should not regard Jesus' use of preaching as unusual in the Greco-Roman world which was accustomed to the street preaching of traveling philosophers, and public orations when the occasion warranted it. Not all, however, were as skilled as the picture we have of Jesus would indicate. He was followed by great crowds, sometimes having to seek a retreat in the countryside. Luke notes that on the occasion when he spoke the parable of the sower "a great crowd came together and people from town after town came to him" (8:4). And in the account of the feeding of the five thousand the crowds had followed him, "and he welcomed them and spoke to them of the kingdom of God" (9:11).

Some of this large following was no doubt due to his reputation as a healer, but there are also indications that his preaching of the "good news" created more than the usual reaction. Luke states that Jesus taught in the synagogues and was *"glorified by all"* (4:15), and Matthew comments at the close of what we call the Sermon on the Mount that "When Jesus finished these sayings, *the crowds were astonished at his teaching"* (7:28; italics mine)—in the face of these comments Jesus' speaking ability must have been marked. Jesus was an outdoor preacher; he had none of the electronic speaking aids to which we are accustomed today. And yet he was heard by multitudes. The quality of his voice, gestures, and facial expressions are unknown to us; yet these factors invariably contribute to one's preaching effectiveness. He made an unforgettable impression upon those who heard him.

I have always appreciated the description which A. V. G. Allen gives in the second of his three-volume biography on Phillips Brooks, the torrential preacher of Trinity Church on Copley Square in Boston:

The doors of the anteroom opens, and Mr. Brooks appears in his white flowing robes. There is something almost boyish, yet beautifully sweet and earnest as well, in his face and manner. He is emphatically a manly man, with no sentimental, morbid, sickly notions of life. He is a "muscular Christian" and believes in work and stout-hearted endeavor, and he walks through the earthly and tangible as beholding the things that are invisible and heavenly. All this and more we find in his strong spritual countenance. [3]

If Phillips Brooks made such an impression upon the congregation of Trinity Church in Boston, what must Jesus' impression have been upon the people of Palestine, especially upon the poor, sick, and needy? He also held the attention of the informed in the synagogue, for as Matthew said: "He taught them as one who had authority, and not as their scribes" (7:29).

It was the custom of the scribes of the Pharisees at the synagogue to undergird their remarks with quotations from learned rabbis, much as we use footnotes today to validate a statement. Although Jesus sometimes referred to Old Testament biblical passages, he did not substitute them for the immediacy of his own grasp of truth. His unforgettable phrase: "But I say unto you—" is an announcement that his words were based on his personal, direct experiences of God's will and word. He was no "professional." This is the mark of the true preacher in every generation.

The Environment of Jesus' Preaching

Jesus' preaching was informal rather than studied. This does not mean that it was superficial; instead it was occasional or situational. Did he ever announce a preaching service in advance? We have no record of it, if he did. Some passer-by would make a remark (Matt. 19:3); a man would suddenly ask a question (Mark 10:17); a disciple would confront him with a request (Luke 11:1)—these occurrences would prompt Jesus to preach. The custom of inviting visiting rabbis to speak at the synagogue sometimes gave him an opportunity to preach as he interpreted the Scriptures (Luke 4:16 ff): open opposition at the synagogue also brought forth from him sermonic utterances (Luke 6:6 ff).

The situational character of Jesus' preaching helps to account for its brevity. You might say that he was committed to the short sermon; even the Sermon on the Mount (Matt. 5–7) is brief. It could be read in a few minutes. And, as it is, it probably is a collection of things that Jesus said on a number of occasions. This does not mean that a great sermon was not preached. Some parts of it appear in a different context in the other Gospels,[4] while Luke's version of what may have been the same sermon and is usually called the Sermon on the Plain, is considerably briefer (Luke 6:17-49).

We have already referred to Jesus' preaching opportunities at the synagogues. In his preaching, Paul also made much use of these meeting places because there was to be found here a combination of both worship and teaching. One theory is that the synagogues came into existence during the Exile when the temple was in ruins and the Jews were captives in Babylon. The prophet Ezekiel mentions the meeting of the Jewish elders in his own home while in exile, and this may mark their beginning (Ezek. 8:1; 20:1-3). Ten males were required to organize a synagogue.[5] By the time of Jesus there was a synagogue in most cities and towns in the Greco-Roman world. Even little Nazareth possessed one where we may assume that Jesus attended school as a child and worshiped as an adult.[6]

Why did Jesus attend the synagogue regularly? Luke tells us that it was his custom (4:16) and suggests that he had been doing so while he was being reared. Now that he was an adult it must have been very boresome for him to listen to some of the scriptural interpretations on occasion. Yet this was the synagogue of his fathers; here too were "the lost sheep of the house of Israel" (Matt. 10:6; 15:24). These were his people who shared his own inheritance. They were the children of Israel who had made a covenant with God. Theirs was the promise of the Messiah and the kingdom. Why shouldn't he go to the synagogue?

How long Jesus continued to go to the synagogue there is no way of knowing. There are indications that he was not always welcome, since his interpretations of the law ran counter to the narrow conservatism of the Pharisees. Sometimes there were arguments between him and them; these must have been irritating to the Jews and tragically disappointing to him (Mark 3:1-6; Luke 4:16-30; 6:6-11). It might be said that it was first in the synagogue that it became evident that the nation would not respond officially to his message of the kingdom.

The settings for Jesus' preaching were not limited to the synagogue. It is said that he preached on a hillside (Matt. 5:1; 24:3), inside a home (Luke 5:19), along the highway (Mark 10:17), and while standing in a boat that had been pushed out from the shore (Mark 4:1). We would conclude that this is in no sense a complete listing, but it does indicate that wherever and whenever there was a place and an occasion for preaching, Jesus was ready to proclaim the good news of the gospel.

How Did He Say It?

Gifts come in many kinds of wrappings. Some are ornate, even fussy, while others are formal and lack ornamentation. It is the same with truth. We have already seen that the Bible expresses its preaching message through many media: narratives, poetry, history, prophetic oracles, et cetera.

This is particularly true of the preaching of Jesus; he had a style that was uniquely his own. There was a poetic quality to his words, yet it was not poetry, strictly speaking. It was imaginative and figurative, because he frequently used metaphors, symbolic expressions, and even hyperbole. Take such statements as the following:

If your right eye causes you to sin, pluck it out. . . . If your right hand causes you to sin, cut it off (Matt. 5:29-30).

To him who strikes you on the cheek, offer the other also; and from him who takes away your coat do not withhold even your shirt (Luke 6:29).

Do not give dogs what is holy; and do not throw your pearls before swine, lest they trample them underfoot and turn to attack you (Matt. 7:6).

Beware of false prophets, who come to you in sheep's clothing, but inwardly are ravenous wolves (Matt. 7:15).

Beware of the leaven of the Pharisees (Mark 8:15).

Enter by the narrow gate; for the gate is wide and the way is easy, that leads to destruction (Matt. 7:13).

Render to Caesar the things that are Caesar's, and to God the things that are God's (Mark 12:17).

Consider the lilies of the field, how they grow; they neither toil nor spin; yet I tell you, even Solomon in all his glory was not arrayed like one of these (Matt. 6:28-29).

No one would fall asleep listening to such preaching as this, and it remained in the brain and heart long after one heard it. This is the reason the tradition concerning Jesus was so full and rich when men came to record it.

Parables And More Parables

Outstanding in the preaching of Jesus was his use of parables. Matthew records that "indeed, he said nothing to them without a parable" (13:34). It is necessary to distinguish between parables, fables, and allegories. A fable is a representation of truth in which the characters—animals trees, etc.—act in unnatural ways such as speaking like people, as in Aesop's writings. An allegory is also a representation of truth by symbolic references in which each detail may have a special meaning. Jesus' allegories of the Vine and the Branches, and the Good Shepherd in John's Gospel are illustrations of this (15:1-11; 10:1-18). A parable, contrary to the above, is a representation of truth in story form that is true to life. People act like people, animals like animals, and birds like birds. What is important to note about a parable, however, is that it has a single meaning only; it is what the story *as a whole* says that counts.

Jesus probably did not originate the parable form, although some scholars argue that he did.[7] When David sinned against Uriah by taking his wife and arranging for the Hittite mercenary soldier to be killed, Nathan the prophet came to him with a story about a rich man who took a poor man's pet lamb for his guest's meal, rather than slaughter one of his own. It so enraged David that the king ordered the offender to be killed (II Sam. 12:1-15). Nathan's story was probably a true-to-life parable which was composed for the occasion. David got the point when Nathan said to him: "You are the man" (vs. 7).

Nathan's story may appear to lack the universal outreach of Jesus' parables in that the truths in Jesus' stories can be applied to countless situations in all ages. Yet there is a principle here that fits numerous occasions. In any case we must first of all realize that the parables came out of the specific setting in which Jesus lived, and here is where their meaning must first be sought. As C. H. Dodd has emphasized, it is the setting in life (*Sitz im Leben*) which is significant in interpreting the parables. *This includes, however, not only the setting at the time Jesus was speaking, but also the setting at the time the parable was being recorded.*[8]

In order to preach in parables one must first of all think in parables. It was because Jesus really believed that heaven was God's throne and *the earth his footstool* (Matt. 5:34-35*a*) that he could find God in all of life and thus speak in parables. Everything he saw—the sea, men fishing, birds, flowers, men farming, women baking and grinding grain, money, filial love, robbers, acts of mercy, marriage feasts, shepherding—all of life reminded him of God. He could not live except in the reality of God's surrounding presence, not only because of his conscience but also because of his vision and insight. Communing with God was like seeing and hearing what was going on around him. Little wonder that he spoke with sorrow about those who had eyes but did not see and ears but did not hear (Mark 8:18).

One could almost construct the complete teachings of Jesus on the basis of the parables alone. Nearly every area of experience and every subject in his preaching was touched upon, directly or indirectly, in his parables. The kingdom, prayer, earthly goods, Christian growth, forgiveness, preparedness, use of personal talents, the meaning of history, friendship, God's character, nature, judgment, the end of the age—all these themes and more are found in his parables.

It is amazing that such an extensive use of stories—for that is what a parable essentially is—did not make Jesus' teachings childish and superficial. When we hear them read or read them ourselves we never feel that he is "talking down" to us. One reason is that they deal with the great themes of human existence. Another is that they are not artificial but true to experience. And a third is Jesus' creative ability. He could do it where others failed.

Jesus' Use of the Old Testament in His Preaching

Jesus' use of the Bible in his preaching is evident in all the Gospels, even as is the use of the Scriptures by the Gospel writers themselves in interpreting the story they are telling. That Jesus did not own any biblical scrolls may be assumed. Few synagogues possessed all of them, and it is hardly likely that one of Jesus' economic status could have afforded any. Yet he showed a familiarity with Old Testament sayings and situations that is unusual.

Jesus probably owed much of his Bible knowledge to hearing it read regularly in the synagogue. Only the law and the Prophets had been accepted as canon by this time, although other scrolls were no doubt also being used. The law in particular dominated Jewish practice in Jesus' day, largely because of its recognition as canon and the influence of the Pharisees, who were exceedingly prominent and stressed its significance for their daily life and national destiny.

Jesus once said of the law: "It is easier for heaven and earth to pass away, than for one dot of the law to become void" (Luke 16:17), and expressed his determination not to destroy it but to fulfill it. The Jewish scholar David Flusser, in line with Jesus' statement, emphasized the fact that when Jesus seems to be denying the validity of the law, he is often simply criticizing the interpretation given to it by the Pharisees.[9]

In quoting from the Bible as he preached, Jesus was not a literalist; he identified with the biblical situation rather than with the verbal statement. Sometimes he preferred one Old Testament passage to another when dealing with the same theme, as in the case of divorce, where he favored Gen. 1:27 and 2:24 to the usual favorite of the Pharisees in Deut. 24:1-4.

Jesus used his Old Testament widely, although he seemed to quote more from some books than others. According to the frequency of the references to them he favored, in order: Isaiah, Deuteronomy, the Psalms, Leviticus, Hosea, Zechariah, Genesis, Exodus, Daniel, I Samuel, Numbers, Nehemiah, and Jeremiah. And his favorite biblical personalities, judged by his naming of them were Abel, Abraham, Isaac, Jacob, Moses, Noah, Jonah, Lot and his wife, David, Solomon, the queen of Sheba, Elijah, Elisha, the widow of Zarephath, and Naaman.[10]

Preaching the Kingdom

The message of the preacher and the preaching itself go hand in hand. If the message is a great truth and the preacher is moved by it, convinced that this is what God wants presented at this particular time, the chances are that he will be inspired to speak with fervor and conviction. We have all heard, however, preaching which did not seem to make any difference to the person preaching. Why should it make a difference to us?

Emil Ludwig, the biographer, held the opinion that no one could write the story of a person's life unless he had a passionate, furious, and mad relationship with his subject.[11] In this light we might point to Jesus' absorbing preoccupation with the theme of the kingdom of God. One can sense this in the enthusiastic announcement with which he began his preaching ministry: "The time if fulfilled, and the kingdom of God is at hand; repent, and believe in the gospel" (Mark 1:15). At another time he said: "The kingdom of God is in the midst of you" (Luke 17:20-21). Still again he announced: "But if it is by the finger of God that I cast out demons, then the kingdom of God has come upon you" (Luke 11:20). He even spoke of men taking it "by force" in his own day (Matt. 11:12). And at the very close of his life, realizing that the kingdom had not yet come in its fullness, he promised the disciples as he established the Lord's supper: "Truly, I say to you, I shall not drink again of the fruit of the vine until that day when I drink it new in the kingdom of God" (Mark 14:25).

The kingdom of God for Jesus was more than a subject or a theme for preaching. It was a long-time expectation among his people, the reign of God, not only over the people of the covenant but over the whole earth. Beginning with hopes of national independence, economic abundance, peace, and victory over the enemies of Israel, it had come at the hands of II Isaiah to be universal in scope as the implications of monotheism impressed him. This prophet, speaking for God, could come to say:

> Thus says the Lord,
> who created the heavens
> (he is God!),

> who formed the earth and made it
> (he established it;
> he did not create it a chaos,
> he formed it to be inhabited!):
> "I am the Lord, and there is no other."
> (45:18)

No cause was of greater significance to Jesus than the kingdom. It was worth more than any man could possess; it was the pearl of great price for which one would sell all other lesser pearls (Matt. 13:45-46), the discovered treasure hidden in the field which was worth the cost of the entire land (Matt. 13:44), and that which one must seek first among all the goals in life (Matt. 6:33).

It was to be expected that in the case of such a tremendous reality men would have different ideas about it. Some of the Jews saw it coming from within the social structure; others viewed it as coming apocalyptically down from the heavens as God overthrew the wicked and blessed the good. The Pharisees believed that the perfect keeping of the law would bring it, especially the Sabbath law.

Various views of the Messiah who would inaugurate the kingdom were also held. There were those who regarded him as a reigning monarch (Isa. 9:6-7; 11:1-10) and others who saw him, either as a suffering individual (suffering servant) for the nation's sake, or as a nation that would be purified through its own suffering. He would bear the sins of mankind by identifying himself with their need (Isa. 52:13–53:12). Still others viewed the Messiah as the glorified Son of man who would come down to earth in apocalyptic splendor to overthrow an evil order and establish a new one (Dan. 7:13-14; see also I Enoch 46:3-4). Jesus' own view probably contained elements of the Suffering Servant as well as of the glorified Son of man.[12]

Jesus' understanding of the kingdom was direct and personal. In essence the kingdom was the rule of God on earth; "thy kingdom come on earth as it is in heaven," Jesus taught men to pray. God's will would be supreme; he would reign in men's hearts forever. What a difference this would make in society!

Sometimes Jesus saw the kingdom as present; again he viewed it as future. Sometimes he spoke of its coming as gradual; again he looked for its sudden arrival in apocalyptic terms, suddenly descending from above. We may take a position on one side or the other as we interpret Jesus' teaching here, or we may conclude that Jesus' view was paradoxical. These ideas are not basically irreconcilable unless we press his thought into a tight system. Besides, it is difficult to determine the extent to which the church interpreted the tradition in reporting it—and the church was quite apocalyptic in its outlook. It is a wonder that the non-apocalyptic view got into the record at all because of this. It must have been very strong. I do not think that we can pin Jesus down to a closely reasoned system of thought. As a preacher he was too much of a poet for such restrictions.

Jesus continued to preach, even during his last week in Jerusalem. His death on the cross interrupted his kerygmatic ministry. But as the resurrected Christ he is represented as continuing to interpret the meaning of the events that happened, (Luke 24:36 ff; Acts 1:3-11).

To this very hour, mankind can never forget that "Jesus came . . . preaching."

X
The Early Church Communicates the Truth

The early Christian community presents a challenge to the church today. Its accomplishments overshadow our own. When we realize that it collected, carried, and put into writing the story of Jesus, which account would have been lost without their efforts, we can begin to see its importance. More than this, the first Christians by responding to the Resurrection and the advent of the Holy Spirit at Pentecost participated in a fellowship that marked the beginning of the church. Had they not come together in a community of faith, Christianity could not have come into being.

There is more to tell. It was to this early church that the task was given to begin to interpret the meaning of all that happened—the birth, ministry, teaching, death, resurrection, and ascension of Jesus, as well as Pentecost. An uninterpreted fact remains a dead fact, unrelated to and disconnected from the whole of life, to reality. The church did not allow the events of Jesus' life to go uninterpreted. In addition to this the early church undertook a mission whereby the faith was shared, first at home and later abroad.

All of the above lies behind the preaching of the early or primitive church. The story itself is found in the book of Acts. It has been estimated that one-fifth of Acts consists of "speeches." I am referring to them as sermons. Even though they do not have the formal setting of a worship service behind them—and the fact is that they are brief and undeveloped—their purpose is to proclaim the truth of the gospel. Persons were daring to speak for God.

The purpose and essence of these sermons in Acts has been pointedly defined in the following statement of Floyd V. Filson in his book *A New Testament History:* "The 'sermons' of The Acts make clear to the reader that the central interest of the story of The Acts is not in the human actors. It is, rather, in the living Christ, who through the Holy Spirit active in the disciples carries forward his work of winning men to accept the gospel, enter the fellowship of God's people, and so prepare for the coming of God's final Kingdom. The 'sermons' focus attention on the gospel, on Christ and the work of the Spirit, and prevent the reader from regarding the story as just a human venture." [1]

The sermons of the early church as found in Acts are not complete, but are presented as digests or summaries of what was said.[2] Luke, the author of Acts, was not present when they were delivered, therefore it must be assumed that he possessed traditions concerning them which went back to eyewitnesses (See Luke 1:1-4). His own style and technique, as we might expect, is discernible in them. Through them, we can catch the feeling of the living church as it bears its witness to what God has done in Christ. This is true *gospel preaching* in its particular emphasis on the mighty acts of God for man's salvation.

Peter at Pentecost

Peter's sermon at Pentecost might properly be regarded as the most important of all in the New Testament, with the exception of the Sermon on the Mount (Matt. 5–7). This is because it interpreted the meaning of the first coming of the Holy Spirit into the hearts of the followers of Christ.[3] They were waiting in Jerusalem, according to Christ's command, to receive "the promise of the Father" (Acts 1:4). It was the time of the celebration of the Feast of Pentecost. This originally was a primitive harvest festival which, among the Jews, had come to celebrate the giving of the law. Some regard it as the greatest of the three major feasts—Passover, Pentecost, and Tabernacles (Booths), although today we tend to place more emphasis upon Passover because of its association with the death of Jesus.

Jerusalem was probably crowded with Jewish pilgrims who had come to observe the feast. Religious fervor and expectation would have been at high pitch. When the followers of Jesus had this tremendous experience of the coming of the Holy Spirit (Acts 2:1-4), their visible (excitation) and audible (speaking in tongues) reactions attracted much attention, and a great crowd drew near, probably because they were curious to see what was happening. That they did not understand is evident from their comments. Some asked what it all meant and others declared that the participants were "filled with new wine" (2:12-13).

There was one present, however, who knew what it meant. This was Peter. He stood with the eleven (Judas' place had been taken by Matthias) and addressed the crowd. In essence he said that God had kept his word; the promise of the Lord through the prophet Joel (2:28-32) that a day would come when he would pour out his Spirit upon all flesh was being fulfilled *before their very eyes* (Acts 2:14-21).

There was a new element in Peter's sermon that went beyond the Joel prophecy. He said that it was Jesus, the doer of mighty deeds, wonders, and signs, the crucified but resurrected Lord, who had sent the Spirit promised in Joel: "Being therefore exalted at the right hand of God, and having received from the Father the promise of the Holy Spirit, he [the resurrected Christ] has poured out this which you see and hear" (Acts 2:33).

What Peter is really saying is that the Day of the Lord (see Amos 5:18) had come. This was to have been an eschatological event in which God's purpose in creation and history would be realized; evil men and nations would be judged and the true people of God be blessed.[4]

The response to Peter's sermon was electric: "Now when they heard this they were cut to the heart, and said to Peter and the rest of the apostles, 'Brethren, what shall we do?'" (2:37). The reply came quickly; they were to repent and be baptized in the name of Jesus Christ for the forgiveness of their sins. Then they too would receive the Holy Spirit. And this they did; the record says that the number who responded in round figures was 3,000. Thus the church was born, fused into being through the presence of the Holy Spirit whom the resurrected and ascended Christ had sent to them. The coming of the Spirit was an experience also of Christ as Lord, for it was he who had sent him—and who had come—into their lives as a living presence. The New Age or Day of the Lord in their thinking, however, had not fully come, for the church still looked for the parousia or return of Christ to the earth. Yet, as Bultmann has reminded us, "in expecting him as the Coming One they understood themselves as the Congregation of the end of days called by him. For them factually—no matter to what degree it may have been clearly conscious—the old had passed away and the world had become new." [5] This is the meaning of Pentecost.

Peter in Solomon's Portico

How did Christian preachers act when in danger of arrest? What did they say at such times? The New Testament represents them as in every sense faithful to their calling. They do not, because of fear, deny their faith, but forthrightly proclaim the gospel. Paul did this when he spoke to the mob in Jerusalem (Acts 22:2 ff) and again in his hearing, while still a prisoner, before King Agrippa at Caesarea (Acts 26:1 ff). It is sometimes said that in conflict the best defense is a strong offensive movement. This theory is illustrated in the early church by preachers who used persecution, even imprisonment, as an occasion to preach.

Peter's sermon to the crowd which gathered after the healing of the lame man (Acts 3:1-10) is just such an instance (Acts 3:11-26). Although it led to his immediate arrest, he continued to preach Jesus. His situation was similar to that of Pastor Niemöller in Berlin who did not hold back but preached the gospel in the presence of Nazi officers, sent to secure evidence against him. This ultimately led to his arrest and imprisonment, but his voice could not be stopped.

In Peter's sermon to "all the people" who gathered about him, he stressed several points. He first of all said that the healing did not occur because of his personal "power or piety." Then in a brief summary he referred to the fact that behind it all was the "God of Abraham and of Isaac and of Jacob, the God of our fathers" (Acts 3:13). He had sent his servant, Jesus, whom they had delivered up in the presence of Pilate. Furthermore they had denied the Holy and Righteous One, asking for a murderer instead. They then killed the Author of life whom God raised from the dead. This is not hearsay, for "to this we are witnesses" (vs. 15b).

What conclusion does Peter draw from all this? Preacher that he was, he interpreted what it meant. He told the people that they had acted in ignorance; the prophets had foretold that the Christ would suffer. They therefore should repent, find forgiveness, and look for "times of refreshing . . . from the presence of the Lord" (3:19). Christ, he added, will return at God's appointed time. They were "sons of the prophets and the covenant," he said. Now, therefore, they should turn from their wickedness.

The names given to Jesus in this sermon indicate that they thought of him in the highest terms, and related his coming and death to God's plan and purpose which he had revealed to the prophets. Jesus is God's *servant* (3:13, 26), *the Holy and Righteous One* (3:14), and the Author of life (3:15).[6] Each of them suggest activity—salvation activity. These sermons of the early church are not generalized discussions of Christian ideals, but references to God's mighty acts in the past, in the present, and in the future. And Christ is the culmination and center of it all. Their character raises the issue of what should be central in Christian preaching today.

Peter at Caesarea

Another of Peter's sermons that has considerable historical and evangelical significance is found in the words he addressed to Cornelius, the Gentile centurion, and to those gathered with him in his home at Caesarea. Even though Peter was a disciple of Jesus who taught God's love for all men, his Jewish background still kept him from feeling completely comfortable with Gentiles. It took two visions and a pressing invitation to get him to go to Caesarea (10:1-33). He only decided to baptize the centurion and those with him because while he was preaching his sermon the Holy Spirit came upon them, Gentiles though they were, just as he had come upon the Jewish pilgrims at Pentecost. Peter was amazed at this turn of events (10:45-48) and proceeded to baptize the group. His defense to himself and to the church when this act was questioned (11:15-17; 15:8-9) was that in baptizing them he was responding to God's initiative in sending upon them the Spirit.[7]

One of the unique notations in this account of Peter's visit to the home of Cornelius is that the Holy Spirit "fell upon all who heard the word" *while the apostle was still preaching to them* (10:44). This seemed to break up the meeting for Peter left off speaking and baptized them. What kind of preaching would bring such results?

Peter's sermon is reported to us by Luke, most probably in outline form (Acts 10:34-43). It is regarded by many biblical scholars as a significant prototype of early Christian preaching. These are the elements, ideas, and emphases which had been accepted as valid. In one sense Peter's words here constitute a type of kerygma, such as might even have been originally used as the basis for constructing the gospel.[8]

Note the points in Peter's sermon:

1. The Word is the "good news" of peace by Jesus Christ.
2. The Word was proclaimed throughout all Judea, beginning from Galilee, after the baptism which John preached.
3. God anointed Jesus of Nazareth with the Holy Spirit and with power.

4. Jesus went about doing good and healing all that were oppressed by the devil.
5. God was with Jesus.
6. Jesus was hanged on a tree [crucified].
7. God raised him up on the third day and made him manifest to a chosen group.
8. They ate and drank with him after the Resurrection.
9. The apostles were commanded to preach that Jesus was the one God has chosen to be judge of the living and the dead.
10. The prophets bear witness to this.
11. All who believe in him receive forgiveness of sins through his name.
12. The apostles are witnesses to these things.

It may be assumed that Peter elaborated upon these points as he preached his sermon. They are the essential ones in telling the story of Jesus, in interpreting God's purpose in these events, and in defining the salvation that comes to those who believe in him. Did Peter first formulate this preaching outline? Did it come from *within* the Christian community which was experiencing the new life in Christ? How much of Peter's own experience is found in these words? How basic is all this for preaching today? These are important questions which the living church must continually seek to answer.

Stephen Before the Council

Stephen was one of "the seven" chosen to administer the common fund to widows, orphans, and the poor, and thus free the apostles of this responsibility so that they could devote their entire time to preaching or "the ministry of the word" (Acts 6:1-6). It seemed to be an excellent idea in principle, but both Philip, also one of the seven, and Stephen became aggressively evangelistic. The former went to Samaria where his preaching led to a revival; the latter preached in the Hellenistic synagogues in Jerusalem which had been provided for nonresidents. It was a service to Hellenists or Jews who lived abroad so they would have a synagogue of their own when they visited the Holy City. Stephen, himself a Hellenistic Jew (Alexandria or Cyrene?), spoke, argued, and debated in these centers. There were probably four with which he was associated— -those of the Freedman (slaves set free), the Cyrenian Jews, the Alexandrian Jews, and the Cilician Jews (Acts 6:9).[9]

Since Stephen was the first Christian martyr, it seemed important to Luke to carry an account of the matters that led to his death. Even though Stephen was a person of "grace and power," he was a provocative speaker and took positions that led to heated arguments and disputes. The chief source of irritation was that he seemed to be downgrading the significance of the temple and Jerusalem (vss. 11-14). Impressions had spread that Stephen spoke blasphemy against the law and even God.

At this point in the record Luke includes a speech or sermon of Stephen's that seems to move awkwardly from point to point, yet it contains a brief for his contention that *there were other places besides the temple and Jerusalem where God spoke to the great men of Israel's past.* Abraham had seen God's glory both in Mesopotamia and Haran (Acts 7:1-8); Joseph had prospered and been providentially cared for in Egypt, even to the saving of the lives of his family (7:9-16). Moses had been instructed in the wisdom of the Egyptians, and in the far land of Midian to which he had fled, sons were born to him. (7:17-29). In that distant land he had seen the burning bush and received God's call to deliver Israel from slavery (7:30-34). And in the days following the exodus from Egypt, Moses had received the law (living oracles) on Mount Sinai and been given instructions in building the tabernacle, the tent of worship. Then Joshua had been victorious in driving out the tribes of Canaan (7:35-45). All this had happened *beyond the borders of Jerusalem and the temple.* One did not need to go to a specific site to find God or be found by him.

It was only *after* these great events in which God dealt with Israel that the ark was taken to Jerusalem by David, and Solomon allowed to build the temple (7:46-47). Therefore they should remember, said Stephen, that "the Most High does not dwell in houses made with hands" (7:48).[10] With a biblical quote, Stephen finished his sermon.

At this point Stephen suddenly burst forth with incendiary words charging the Jews with being stiff-necked, uncircumcised in heart, and resisting both the Holy Spirit and the prophets. He also accused them of murdering Jesus, the Righteous One. On top of all this he said that they did not keep the law which was "delivered by angels" (7:51-53). The result of this scathing denunciation was sheer tragedy, for by it a furious and murderous mob action was set into motion and Stephen was stoned (7:54-60).

G. H. C. Macgregor has said that "had Stephen lived he would have ranked with the greatest of the apostles. . . . Stephen's significance is that his preaching in the Hellenistic synagogues made it evident that Christianity was something more than just a new Jewish sect. . . . He drove the first wedge between Judaism and Christianity and made possible the emergence of a distinctively Christian church." [11] Quite an accomplishment, and preaching was his weapon!

XI
Paul Proclaims Salvation

No preacher, except Jesus, has had as great an influence upon Christianity and Christians as Paul of Tarsus, who said that by virtue of his experience of Christ and his suffering in Christ's service he deserved to be called an apostle (II Cor. 11:1–12: 13). So great has been this influence that he has been accused of turning the simple religion of Jesus into an involved theological system which is often called Paulinism or the Faith of Paul.

On the surface Paul appears to know little about the earthly life of Jesus. This is because he does not refer often to the details of his ministry, but stresses instead what God in Christ has done for men who stand in need of righteousness which they have been unable to find, either through the Jewish law or through the religious practices of the Gentiles. Whether he had actually seen Jesus in the flesh is conjectural; he had, however, numerous contacts with those who did, and also with those who experienced the Resurrection.

The Making of a Preacher

Every man who speaks for God as Paul does has a story to tell concerning his call and commission to this ministry. Bishop Edwin Holt Hughes chose as the title of his autobiography the statement, "I was made a minister." Paul could have selected similar words to describe his own background. He tells us about it in several brief summaries. The first of these which we shall quote says:

> For I would have you know, brethren, that the gospel which was preached by me is not man's gospel. For I did not receive it from man, nor was I taught it, but it came *through a revelation of Jesus Christ*. For you have heard of my former life in Judaism, how I persecuted the church of God violently and tried to destroy it; and I advanced in Judaism beyond many of my own age among my people, so extremely zealous was I for

the traditions of my fathers. But when he who had set me apart before I was born, and had called me through his grace, was pleased to reveal his Son to (in) me *in order that I might preach him* among the Gentiles, I did not confer with flesh and blood, nor did I go up to Jerusalem to those who were apostles before me, but I went away into Arabia; and again I returned to Damascus. (Gal. 1:11-17; italics mine.)

This statement was written in one of the first of Paul's letters. He is most aggressive as he writes because the churches in the Galatian area which he had founded, probably on his first missionary journey (Acts 13–14),[1] were being misled by the Judaizers who had infiltrated them and who were attempting to undercut the doctrine Paul had preached of salvation by faith. These Jewish Christians who were urging circumcision or Gnostic practices for converts were creating a serious disturbance among the Galatian Christians which threatened their joy and freedom in Christ. Paul insisted that they return to his gospel of salvation by faith which had come to him by *revelation.*

The second statement of Paul concerning his experience in becoming a preacher of Christ which we shall quote comes from Philippians, one of his latest letters, if not actually his last one. It is one of his prison epistles in which he is writing to his most faithful church.[2] Here again we can see in the background persons or groups who were disturbing the church with false doctrine, possibly Judaizers within the church, Jews themselves, or even Jewish Christians with Gnostic views.[3] In any case, the apostle undergirds his advice to hold out against this false teaching (Phil. 3:2-3) by referring to his own background, telling them why and how he became a preacher. He is one worthy of their confidence. They should not trust such acts as circumcision for their salvation. He did not do this, although he had plenty of reasons to do so:

If any other man thinks he has reason for confidence in the flesh, I have more: circumcised on the eighth day, of the people of Israel, of the tribe of Benjamin, a Hebrew born of Hebrews; as to the law a Pharisee, as to zeal a persecutor of the church, as to righteousness under the law blameless. But whatever gain I had, I counted as loss for the sake of Christ. Indeed I count everything as loss because of the surpassing worth of knowing Christ Jesus my Lord (Phil. 3:4b-8a).

Paul's background, so briefly sketched above, would have been envied by any serious-minded Jew. There were few, if any, who could surpass it. He had been born in Tarsus, a city of Cilicia (Acts 21:39). Famous as a center of learning and a seat of Stoicism it provided the best in Hellenistic culture. What effect all this had upon Paul would be difficult to assess. Although there are some philosophical overtones to his preaching, by and large, his gospel was proclaimed and interpreted as over against a Hebrew background. He had become a Pharisee, having, it is said, studied under Gamaliel at Jerusalem (Acts 22:3; 26:4).

The mention of Paul's activities in persecuting the Christians in the above quotations is significant. This determination to wipe out the opposition was excessive in its zeal. Other Jews disliked and disagreed with the Christian practice and preaching quite as much as Paul, but did not exercise such aggressiveness in opposing it. This same capacity and energy, however, once it was reversed and put to work on behalf of Christ, carried the gospel far and wide in the Greco-Roman world and produced almost half of the New Testament itself.

Primarily, Paul's persecution activities were motivated by his reaction against the affirmations by the Christians that Jesus was the Messiah. The other teachings of the church were not too different from his own. Jews and Christians alike accepted the Old Testament, except for the fact that now for the latter something new had been added. Jesus had by his crucifixion and resurrection opened a way of salvation that challenged and even replaced the centrality of the law. He was truly the Lord.

Does not this help to explain Paul's conversion experience in which he heard Jesus say: "Saul, Saul, why do you persecute *me"* (Acts 9:4; italics mine)? It was Jesus himself against whom Paul was fighting as he persecuted the Christians. Once he found and surrendered to Jesus as Lord in this ecstatic moment, the direction of his basic drive was reset. Faith in Christ became central in Paul's thinking, preaching, and actions, and supplanted the law as a way to righteousness.

Paul Preached a Way of Salvation

Christianity is a salvation religion. It is concerned with ethics and what we may loosely call Christian culture because it is related to life. But over and above this, its chief function as spelled out by Paul is to bring men to God. He has already come to them in Christ; they are left with the responsibility of receiving God's gift by faith.

In preaching a way of salvation Paul was following the thrust of the Old Testament with which he was already familiar. Discovering a way of salvation in Christianity, therefore, was not something new for him. Its newness came in its focus on what God had done, was now doing, and was yet to do in Christ.

Paul deals with many themes in his letters, but whatever the subject—marriage, charismatic gifts, eating meat offered to idols, the incarnation, the end of the age, love, suffering, death, the Resurrection, the Holy Spirit—in each and every word his concern is salvation, new life in Christ. James D. Smart writes of this being "in Christ," and says: "To be in Christ is to have the 'mind' of Christ, to see all things from a new vantage point, to do one's thinking from a new center . . ." [4] Paul wrote: "If anyone is in Christ, he is a new creation; the old has passed away; behold, the new has come. All this is from God, who through Christ reconciled us to himself and gave us the ministry of reconciliation" (II Cor. 5:17-18). Both are saying the same thing in spite of the fact that nearly two thousand years separate the two.

That Paul spent his life as a Christian in preaching is abundantly clear from the New Testament. In the account of his missionary activities in the book of Acts there are frequent references to this activity as well as specific sermons that he preached. Some of these in the record were the ones delivered at Antioch (in Pisidia), Lystra, and Athens. In addition to these we have numerous epistles in the New Testament which are customarily assigned to him directly or indirectly.[5] Because they are letters we must ask in what sense these epistles are sermonic. Under what circumstances does a letter become a sermon?

Usually we think of a sermon solely as an oral utterance within the framework of the Christian faith for the purpose of evangelizing, instructing, or encouraging persons. It is my position here, however, that a written statement expressed with conviction and inspiration, and directed to the same goal as a spoken sermon, may also be regarded as sermonic. Therefore in considering Paul as one proclaiming salvation, we shall include both his reported sermons in Acts and also passages from his letters to the churches.

Paul's Sermons In Acts
At Antioch

The sermons of Paul recorded in the book of Acts are well adapted to the situations in which they were preached and the issue or theme to which he was speaking.[6] At Antioch in Pisidia, the apostle was preaching in the synagogue, mostly to Jews, and therefore he addresses himself to them according to their own outlook (Acts 13:16b-41). He first gives a brief summary of Hebrew history to the time of David, and then passes over to Jesus whom he presents as the Savior descended from David who had been promised to Israel. Then follows a summary of Jesus' arrest, crucifixion, and resurrection. He regards all this as fulfilling prophecy, and urges his hearers to trust the Lord for forgiveness and be freed from the law of Moses. This is the kind of sermon Paul would have preached to a Jewish congregation. It was so effective that the response of the people made the Jewish leaders at the synagogue jealous (vs. 45).

At Lystra

At Lystra, however, the apostle was preaching to pagan Gentiles. Paul had healed a man who had been lame from birth (14:8-18). So greatly impressed were the natives that they cried: "The gods have come down to us in the likeness of men!" (14:11). They called Barnabas *Zeus* and Paul *Hermes* and brought out oxen and garlands to sacrifice to them. How religious! How superstitious! Paul tore his garments to express his disapproval and rushed into the midst of the crowd, attempting to preach to them in order to deter them.

His sermon, unlike that in Antioch, made no mention of Jewish prophecies or the law of Moses. These persons would not have understood nor been impressed. Instead, he stressed the blessings of nature by which the living God had given them rain and fruitful seasons and had brought happiness to their hearts. This was a pertinent approach, but so great was their excitement that they interrupted and wanted to continue their sacrifice; Paul did not even get to mention Christ. In the end their love turned to hate and they stoned the apostle instead of worshiping him (vs. 19).

At Athens

Paul's sermon at Athens (17:22-31) was a masterful attempt to relate himself to the people about him. As you stand today on the large mass of rock which was probably the Areopagus (Mars Hill), where the citizens of the city used to address their fellows, and look up in an easterly direction you will see the entrance to the Acropolis, several hundred feet above. There you will view the ruins of the temples which were built for the worship of the Greek gods. Their size and magnificence even in their state of decay today will overpower you. In Paul's day they were intact and presented a view of architectural splendor unequaled in the world. It was this sight probably that provided the background for the apostle's opening statement in his sermon: "Men of Athens, I perceive that in every way you are very religious." [7]

How religious the Athenians were! It makes one sad to see this devotion to false gods. Surely Paul had this same reaction and began to present a philosophical rationale for the faith he proclaimed. Some Epicureans, followers of Epicurus (*ca.* 300 B.C.), and Stoics, followers of Zeno (*ca.* 300 B.C.) were among his crowd of listeners (17:18). Both stressed happiness according to nature, so that Paul's words in his sermon concerning creation, geography, and the national groupings of people were highly appropriate (17:24-26). The apostle even quotes from contemporary poets with reference to man's life in God: "In him we live and move and have our being." He closes the quotations by including one from another source which refers to man as God's offspring.[8]

As was noted above, Paul held the attention of his audience with this line of reasoning, but when he came to morality and the final judgment, and proclaimed the reality of the Resurrection they turned away, some mocking and others saying that they would hear the apostle again. Whether they did or not, we cannot say, but it is clear that no Christian church was founded at Athens. This does not mean that Paul failed because he preached philosophy rather than Christ, as some would conclude on the basis of I Cor. 2:2, where he tells the Corinthians (whom he visited following his stay in Athens) that he came among them determining to preach Christ only. I regard Paul's sermon as particularly relevant to the situation he found at Athens. It was the moral indifference and intellectual sophistication of his audience (vs. 21) that caused them to turn a deaf ear to his words just as he seemed about to mention Christ by name.

Paul's Sermonic Letters

I stated earlier in this chapter that there were sermonic elements in Paul's letters. This is evidenced by their fervor and direct appeal to the church which led them to amend their ways and turn to Christ. Paul usually, if not always, dictated his letters to one of his associates. At the close he usually added personal greetings in his own hand, and signed it so that it would carry the authority of his personal signature (I Cor. 16: 21; Colossians 4:18; II Thess. 3:17; Philem. vs. 19; Gal. 6:11).

Anyone who has ever dictated to a secretary has probably, at some time or other, stopped in his tracks and paused while elaborating emotionally on a certain point he was making. Such words usually had a special character. It is wholly suppositional, but is it not likely that Paul did the same thing as he wrote to the churches? He knew these persons, except probably the recipients of the book of Romans, and had close feelings of affection and concern for them. There was always an issue at stake, usually a very personal one; this would invite strong verbal exhortation, tantamount to preaching.

There are numerous passages in Paul's letters where expressions of feeling and concern, appeal, and warning reach such heights that one can almost hear the apostle's voice, see his stance, and observe his countenance. Frequently they appear following a discussion of a major Christian issue.

Death As Victory

In Paul's first letter to the Corinthians the apostle had been facing the question of the Christian's hope of life after death. Some in the church had denied belief in immortality—a point of view unthinkable to him (I Cor. 15:12-19): "If for this life only we have hoped in Christ, we are of all men most to be pitied" (vs. 19). Others were concerned with the nature of the body we shall have in the next life. Paul brilliantly by analogy argued that it will be a spiritual body (I Cor. 15:42-50). At the close of his statement he was so caught up in faith in immortality that he cried out exultantly:

When the perishable puts on the imperishable, and the mortal puts on immortality, then shall come to pass the saying that is written:
"Death is swallowed up in victory."
"O death, where is thy victory?
O death, where is thy sting?"
The sting of death is sin, and the power of sin is the law. *But thanks be to God, who gives us the victory through our Lord Jesus Christ.*

(I Cor. 15:54-57; italics mine.)

Christ Holds Us in Love Forever

Another illustration of sermonic exclamation is found in Paul's letter to the Romans. The apostle had been spelling out the blessing and power that comes to one in whom the Spirit of Christ dwells (Rom. 8:9-30). He knows that he has the freedom of a son (vs. 14), that the Spirit brings him strength by praying in him or for him (vss. 26-27), and that God can put all the facts of his life together for good (vs. 28).

In the face of all this, Paul is overcome with a tremendous sense of God's love in Christ, and he asks triumphantly: "If God is for us, who is against us? He who did not spare his own Son but gave him up for us all, will he not also give us all things with him?" (vss. 31-32). But this is only the beginning. The apostle continues in a flow of inspired words such as characterizes great preaching:

Who shall separate us from the love of Christ? Shall tribulation, or distress, or persecution, or famine, or nakedness, or peril or sword? . . . No, in all these things we are more than conquerors through him who loved us. For I am sure that neither death, nor life, nor angels, nor principalities, nor things present, nor things to come, nor powers, nor height, nor depth, nor anything else, in all creation, will be able to separate us from the love of God in Christ Jesus our Lord (vss. 35-39).

What a heightened sense of divine providence as it centers in "the love of God in Christ Jesus our Lord"!

The Mystery of God's Wisdom

There is yet another tremendous sermonic passage that brings to a close Paul's attempt to answer the question as to why the Jews rejected Jesus, the Messiah, when he came (Rom. 9–11). Paul's answer contained three points: (1) Not all did reject him; some Jews believed. (2) The refusal of the Jews was God's way of opening the door to Gentiles. (3) At the end the Jews will return to the fold together with the Gentiles; they will once more be grafted into the vine.

This was a thoughtful answer, but it did not finally satisfy Paul. Unanswered questions remained. But the fact of God, his wisdom and knowledge, were real and sure. He will bring the problem to a glorious solution, and so Paul exclaims:

O the depth of the riches and wisdom and knowledge of God! How unsearchable are his judgments and how inscrutable his ways!

> "For who has known the mind of the
>   Lord,
> or who has been his counselor?"
> "Or who has given a gift to him
> that he might be repaid?"

For from him and through him and to him are all things. To him be glory for ever. Amen.

(Rom. 11:33-36; italics mine.)

In this impressive climax there are reflections of Old Testament verses.[9] Paul's scriptures came to his aid in phrasing what may be regarded as one of the most elevated statements of worship in all of his letters. This was a spontaneous rather than a studied utterance. It is sheer praise.

Salvation Is the Goal

It has already been noted in this chapter that Christianity is a salvation religion.[10] This message is portrayed in a number of ways in the New Testament. In the Synoptic Gospels salvation is related to the near advent of the kingdom of God; it was actually present for those who were united to God through Christ. But it was still to come in its fullness. The Gospel of John interprets this salvation as eternal life, which again comes through one's relationship to Christ.

Paul gives us an interpretation of salvation in terms of man's being forgiven and declared righteous before God. This he presents in numerous statements, some of which are highly sermonic in character as though they were delivered from a pulpit.

Take the following statement from Colossians: "He [God] has delivered us from the dominion of darkness and transferred us to the kingdom of his beloved Son, in whom we have redemption, the forgiveness of sins" (1:13-14). Here is another from Colossians: "And you, who once were estranged and hostile in mind, doing evil deeds, he has now reconciled in his [Christ] body of flesh by his death, in order to present you holy and blameless and irreproachable before him" . . . (1:21-22). One cannot miss the surge of a great declaration in such words.

A Theological Basis for Salvation

Paul's letters are largely situational in character. He had his eyes and heart fixed on the living church. Theology is here, no doubt about it. But it is present not so much to develop and present a system of thought as to help persons find salvation in

Christ. Even the book of Romans, which is more ostensibly theological than the others, was written to prepare the way for a visit of the apostle so that when he arrived he could be immediately helpful. The church there would know what he believed and what would be the basis of his preaching.

Theology, per se, was not Paul's major concern; he was a preaching missionary first of all. It is as Frank W. Beare has said of Paul's works: "They are intensely personal; and if you read them in this spirit, you will find that they have an extraordinary liveliness and vigor." [11] These letters were *vocally dictated,* and intended to be *vocally read.* This explains in part why they are not formal theological treatises but are sermonic in character. Had Paul been present in person he would probably have spoken just as his letters sound.[12] This does not mean that Paul was disorganized in his thinking, although he does sometimes seem to be moved more by impulse than by logical development.

Salvation Presented in Romans

Paul's theological thinking is presented in a more or less orderly way in the book of Romans. He had not yet visited this church, in spite of the unusually large number of personal names he mentions in chapter 16.[13] General truths of the Faith were, therefore, about all that Paul could present in writing to the Roman community in Christ.

The following brief outline, which in itself could be the basis of an extended sermon, underlies Paul's presentation of salvation in the book of Romans:

I.   Introduction (1:1-17)
II.   All, Jews and Gentiles, have sinned and are under God's judgment (1:18–3:20)
III. Salvation is provided in Christ by faith (3:21-31)
IV.   Abraham was saved by faith (4:1-25)
V.   The blessedness of the justified (5:1-21)

Basic to Paul's line of thought in Romans is his conviction, growing out of his personal experience, that salvation could not be had through the law. The law could define what was good and right but could not empower man to achieve it. Therefore God in sending Christ opened a way whereby through faith in him man is accepted on the basis, not of works, but of faith. Here is such freedom as a prisoner before a court of law experiences when, although not perfect, he is declared to be not guilty (justification); here is such freedom as a slave experiences who is given his freedom by his master (redemption); here is such freedom as one knows when he trusts the sacrifice on the altar, a sacrifice in which only Christ's blood can bring atonement (expiation)[14] (see Rom. 3:21-26).

This great salvation described above leads Paul to make a number of sermonic appeals. He wants men to respond to what God has done in Christ. He urges them to consider themselves "dead to sin and alive to God" (6:11), and counsels them not to yield their "members to sin as instruments of wickedness," but instead to yield themselves "to God *as men who have been brought from death to life*" (6:13; italics mine). Paul reaches a climax in sermonic exhortation when he says: "I appeal to you therefore, brethren, by the mercies of God, to present your bodies as a living sacrifice, holy and acceptable to God, which is your spiritual worship," and adds: "Do not be conformed to this world but be transformed by the renewal of your mind, that

you may prove what is the will of God, what is good and acceptable and perfect" (12:1-2). Surely Paul the preacher is to be
seen in these words.

Love—the Crown of Salvation

The thirteenth chapter of I Corinthians is perhaps Paul's most
famous passage. It is often called the "love song" of the New
Testament. Not only because of its message, but also because of
its literary merit, it is widely read and even incorporated in
fraternal rituals. Sometimes it is suggested that this poem is
Paul's portrait of Christ.

These words on love come at the close of a discussion on
spiritual gifts which the Holy Spirit gives to men. The gifts
varied in their appeal since some were more spectacular than
others and, therefore, seemed more desirable. After attempting
by the use of the analogy of the human body in which there
are numerous parts, great and small, and all are needed for the
well-being of the whole, Paul, the preacher, makes a personal
appeal: "I will show you a still more excellent way" (12:31b).
He then proceeds to tell them that love is the greatest of all
gifts, and that everyone of them could possess it.

Where does one begin to point out the glory of love as
presented by Paul when he urges men to seek it out rather
than to quibble over which of the charismatic gifts they preferred? He says that love outlasts and outstrips all other gifts.
It expresses itself through patience, kindness, humility, and
courtesy. Paul concludes that "faith, hope, love abide, these
three; but the greatest of these is love" (13:13).[15] He immediately adds: "Make love your aim" (14:1).

XII
The Later Church Confronts
Its Age

It is sobering to realize that those who spoke for God in the Bible were not dealing in vague generalities but were confronting concrete situations. They were not like Cervantes' Don Quixote who went out, dressed like a knight, to joust with windmills. This crazed Spanish country gentleman has become a symbol of those who are unrealistic in the fight against evil. He meant well, but his world was an illusion. Not so with the preachers in the later church.

When men like the authors of I Peter, Hebrews, the book of Revelation, and the Epistle of James wrote their books, they were actually striking out at critical and sensitive situations, both within and without the church. Heresy, false doctrine, persecution, threats to the Christian character of the life within the church, the relation of the church to the state, the causes of war—all these and other issues were in danger of engulfing the Christian community. How should a Christian act, live, and think in the midst of this kind of world? Attempts to answer such questions in selected writings of this period in the life of the church follow.

I Peter

Date

The letter known as I Peter has traditionally been assigned to the apostle Peter as its author.[1] Its Greek however, is thought by many scholars to be too excellent for a Galilean fisherman.[2] Perhaps, it is countered, that Silvanus was the actual penman while the sentiments were Peter's (5:12). Silvanus had been a companion of the apostle Paul (II Cor. 1:19; I Thess. 1:1; II Thess. 1:1) and would have known how to put Peter's ideas and message into a writing of this character. If Peter wrote it, the date would be in the sixties; if another, it would belong in the

period of the emperor Domitian. There is a background of persecution behind this letter, and the sixties saw Nero as a persecutor, while the nineties witnessed Domitian in the same role.[3]
Its source was Rome (Babylon 5:13), and it was addressed
mostly to Gentile converts (1:14; 2:10; 4:3).

How to Face Suffering

The main purpose of the author of I Peter was to strengthen
and encourage those who were about to face political and social
persecution, even possible martyrdom. How do you do this,
then or now? Peter in speaking for God urges the church to
think upon the sufferings of Christ. They should rejoice as
those who "share Christ's sufferings" (4:13). Then they are
reminded that out of all this a great "glory" is to be revealed
(4:13; 5:1). The end of time is near at hand; he says that it will
not be long now until Christ returns. Keeping their sanity and
remaining sober, praying, and holding "unfailing . . . love for
one another" is to be their daily way of life during these days
of waiting (4:7-8). Finally, he says to the church that this suffering which they are facing is not theirs alone; their brothers
"throughout the world" must meet it also (5:9). What practical guidance this is! In each of these suggestions there is a motivation that is Christian, such as all preaching must involve.

Target Preaching

One of the reasons that is sometimes given to undergird the
conclusion that this letter was not written by the apostle Peter is
that it is lacking in references to the details of the ministry of
Jesus.[4] The author, however, was not writing a gospel. It could
be that he picked out from his memory only the thing in his
Lord's life *that would meet their specific need.* This is "target"
preaching, counseling, or teaching. That one thing was the suffering of Christ himself.

How appealingly he refers to it! "Since therefore Christ suffered in the flesh, arm yourselves with the same thought" (4:1). Add to this Peter's appeal for joy: "But rejoice in so far as you share Christ's sufferings, that you may also rejoice and be glad when his glory is revealed. If you are reproached for the name of Christ, you are blessed, because the spirit of glory and of God rests upon you" (4:13-14). Furthermore, "if one suffers as a Christian, let him not be ashamed, but under that name let him glorify God" (4:16).[5]

Additional Emphases

As a Christian preacher Peter had a tremendous conviction that the Christians were "God's own people." They were unique, special, individual, "a chosen race, a royal priesthood, a holy nation." He told them that they were raised up to "Declare the wonderful deeds of him who called you out of darkness into his marvelous light" (2:9). This is the theme that Peter proclaimed as he spoke for God. Do we think as highly as this of the church today?

Other emphases of Peter were the living hope that came through the Resurrection (1:3), the prophetic references to the sufferings of Christ (1:10-11), obedience to the law and the state (2:13-17), and Christ's preaching in Hades between his death and resurrection (3:18-20). The latter became the scriptural basis for the statement in the Apostles' Creed: "He descended into hell."

Hebrews

Authorship and Date

The Letter to the Hebrews is pseudonymous. Suggested authors include Paul, Barnabas, Apollos, Aquila, Priscilla, Silas, Timothy, and Luke. What a list of great Christians! Because of its conceptual design along the lines of Platonic dualism, Apollos seems a most likely candidate to me since he came from the philosophical-minded city of Alexandria (see Acts 18:24-25) and the writing has a philosophical and theological framework.

Hebrews may be dated somewhere around the year A.D. 90. We can see that Rome had already begun to persecute the Christians (10:32-39); its severity was to grow (12:4). Christians were being tempted to renounce their Faith (3:12; 10:23). These were second-generation Christians (13:7, 17), who needed to persevere and hold fast (3:6); returning from apostasy to belief was exceedingly difficult, if not impossible (6:4-6; 10:26-31).

First Readers

Who were the Hebrews to whom this letter was sent? Were they Palestinians as the numerous references to the tabernacle and old covenant in the writing might suggest? Against this conclusion is the fact that the thought-patterns of the book and its background seem to be Hellenistic.[6] Perhaps the church in Rome may have been the recipient of the letter (13:24). Yet, theologically speaking, the Ephesian church also may have welcomed it first.[7]

Such questions as authorship, date, and the first readers of Hebrews may have to remain open for some time. But the outlines of the message of the author as he spoke for God in offering specific teaching to meet the needs of the living church in that age can be traced in the book as it stands.

Christ's Humanity and Man's Salvation

First of all, Hebrews insists that Jesus was truly human. This is not just a historical or only an anti-Gnostic concern of his. It is also personal and theological. To him Jesus had to be "made like his brethren in every respect, so that he might become a merciful and faithful high priest in the service of God, to make expiation for the sins of the people" (2:17). Why? Only thus could he help the tempted; he, having also been tempted, will understand man's temptations (2:18). Preaching the humanity of Jesus as a basis for atonement (expiation) is a unique insight for this author. Jesus can sympathize with our weakness because he knows our problems firsthand (4:15); this will give us confidence to come before the "throne of grace" (4:16). It is a part of the access he has made possible.

The author of Hebrews sees yet another significance in Jesus' humanity. The Lord Christ not only knew man's struggle with temptation, but was also familiar with what it means and how it feels to die. This too would give man courage. But there is more here than this. In dying, Jesus destroyed "him who has the power of death, that is, the devil" (2:14). Belief in the devil's possessing power over death was held by both Jews and Christians in that day. *Now that that power has been broken, salvation is available for all who believe.*

An Eternal High Priest and a Perfect Sacrifice

The author of Hebrews also sees another side to the nature and work of Jesus; he is the eternal high priest. In presenting Jesus Christ as such a high priest, one who eternally can bring men to God, the author compares the perfection of the heavenly order of sacrifice for sin with its perfect high priest, perfect offering, and once-and-for-all sacrifice, with the imperfect and temporary sacrificial services and practices of the earthly priests and the tabernacle (9:11-12; 10:11-12). And the framework for the comparison between the perfect order (heavenly) and the imperfect (earthly) is found in Platonic dualism. Here in Plato the perfect order of Ideas in heaven is seen in contrast with the imperfect order of their manifestations on earth.[8]

In all of this the writer is confronting contemporary points of view, thought systems, and practices with his gospel, in order to show that Christianity is better. He does some original thinking as he addresses the people by declaring that in Christ there is a new order of the priesthood in contrast to the limited lines of Aaron and of the Levitical priests. It is the order of Melchizedek, king of Salem, a mythical figure who is pictured in Genesis as a priest of the Most High who blessed Abraham (14:17 ff). Having no genealogy he is eternal (Heb. 7:3). Christ's uniqueness as eternal high priest required a new covenant (8:8-13).

A Call to Faith

After presenting an analysis of salvation in Christ, the great high priest, as over against that provided by earthly priests and tabernacle services, the author of Hebrews shows his sermonic interest by turning to the subject of the need for faith. He begins by defining faith as "the assurance of things hoped for, the conviction of things not seen" (11:1). Then he presents a list of the heroic leaders, both in Israel's past and in the Christian fold, who made their way against unbelievable odds and hardships (11:4-40). How? By faith!

Preacher that he is, the author draws his great conclusion and makes his triumphant appeal to the people. He begins by using the word "Therefore," as he introduces a kind of altar call: "Therefore, since we are surrounded by so great a cloud of witnesses, let us also lay aside every weight, and sin which clings so closely, and let us run with perserverance the race that is set before us, looking to Jesus the pioneer and perfecter of our faith, who for the joy that was set before him endured the cross, despising the shame, and is seated at the right hand of the throne of God" (12:1-2).

The Revelation to John

Throughout this extended account of the men who dared to speak for God we have noticed great variety in the individuals who were involved and the procedures that were followed. Narrators, historians, prophets, poets, sages, gospel writers, and those who composed epistles—each has made his own witness in his own way. And the persons who have stood out in the New Testament include Jesus, Peter, and Paul. No two were alike in personality, background, preaching techniques, or style of thinking and writing.

Authorship and Setting

The author of the Revelation to John adds another kind of person to the role; whether he is John the Apostle, a pupil of John's, John the Presbyter, or another unknown ecstatic who experienced visions, there can be no doubt that he had a Word from God to proclaim. I choose to call him John the Seer, because his name was John and he was a seer.[9]

This man spoke for God in a tempestous time. Domitian, the Roman Emperor, was demanding that he be worshiped as a divine being. Other emperors during the first century A.D. had accepted divine honors in a light-hearted way because it flattered them; Domitian, however, in the latter part of his reign (A.D. 96) took it seriously and required it under the threat of punishment or death if it were not done (Rev. 13:11-18). John, the author, had already been imprisoned on the island of Patmos "on account of the word of God and the testimony of Jesus" (1:9). This does not say that his arrest and incarceration were because he refused to practice emperor worship. The reason given was that he spoke out bravely for God as he bore his witness to Jesus. With this background he had the right to call upon others to be loyal in spite of threats, suffering, or death. Had he not done the same?

Method, Message, and Meaning

In bearing his witness to the Christians who were facing this issue through writing the book of Revelation, John expressed himself in symbolic terms. Here was a man who experienced wonderful visions; he was "in the Spirit" from time to time and saw great scenes of heaven and events on earth (1:10; 4:2). He then recorded them in the vernacular of apocalyptic.[10] The numbers 7, 3½, 12, 144,000, etc. had esoteric significance, as did the reference to horns, eyes, stars, and so forth throughout the writing.

As a result of his visions the author promised that the end of the age was coming soon (1:3; 22:6, 7, 12, 20), following a period of judgments. Christ, the warrior Messiah, would return with a heavenly army and overcome all evil nations on earth and forces in the spirit world, including Satan, whom he sees as a dragon. Christ would be King of kings and Lord of lords (19:16). The Christians should hold out against Domitian.

A final judgment would soon take place; the evil would be sent to the "lake of fire," but the faithful would be preserved forever in a "new heaven and a new earth." They would live in the holy city, the new Jerusalem, which would come down from heaven. No light from the sun or the moon would be needed, "for the glory of God [would be] its light, and its lamp [would be] the Lamb" who is Christ (21:23). Here they shall reign for ever and ever (22:5).

No more dramatic message than this has ever been delivered in relation to the struggle between good and evil. To this very hour it reminds us that it is taking place. Realistic preaching this! And it promises the ultimate victory of what is good, of Christ and those who claim him Lord. This was a word from God for these dark days.

The Letter of James

Background

When James speaks for God he does it directly and in a practical manner. It is in its very style a sermon or a homily. In the letter of James, which is highly Jewish in tone, the name of

Christ appears only twice (1:1; 2:1). Some have suggested that it was originally a Jewish writing which had been adapted to Christian usage by a later editor.[11] This is a purely theoretical conclusion, however, and has not met with wide acceptance.

Because the book of James deals largely with matters of conduct and skirts Pauline theology, it has been compared with Jesus' Sermon on the Mount (cf. James 1:6-8; 2:8; and 5:12). An early date has, therefore, been suggested, even before Paul's writings.[12] Yet within the book itself we see a living church which was working out its discipline at a later, more organized period. The author was familiar with Paul's published letters (A.D. 90) and seems to be attempting to offset emphasis upon faith that does not show itself in Christian action and character (James 2:14 ff). This would date it late, *circa* A.D. 100. James most probably lived abroad and may have been a Hellenistic Jew before his conversion to Christianity.[13]

The Preacher and His Message

The author of the letter of James is one who is masterful in his use of analogies and illustrations. He speaks of the wind and the waves of the sea (1:6), reflections in a mirror (1:23), horses and bridles (3:3), ships and rudders (3:4), forest fires (3:5), and farmers (5:7). Theological terminology gives way to such expressions as "the royal law" (2:8) and practical definitions of religion: "Religion that is pure and undefiled before God and the Father is this: to visit orphans and widows in their affliction, and to keep oneself unstained from the world" (1:27).

The message which James proclaims is directed toward the need to put one's religion into practice. If you don't have faith, you are like a wave of the sea which is at the mercy of the wind (1:6). When one is tempted he should realize that his own desires are the cause, not God (1:13-15). One should not only hear the gospel; he should also be a doer (1:22). The rich should not be shown favoritism at the expense of the poor (2:1-7). Hungry and cold persons should be fed and clothed as well as preached to (2:14-17). True faith will express itself in works or deeds (2:18-26). The tongue should be brought under control (3:6-12). War is caused by greed (4:1-3). The future is in God's hand, so be open to his guidance (4:13-17). Patience and steadfastness are Christian virtues (5:7-11). Pray for the sick (5:13-15). And, finally, "Whoever brings back a sinner from the error of his way will save his soul from death and will cover a multitude of sins" (5:20).

James did not live or preach in the clouds. He had two feet on earth at all times, yet he was not wordly or materialistic. A deep faith in God underlies his preaching message. Because of this he could speak for God.

NOTES

I. WHO SPEAKS FOR GOD?

1. Malcolm Boyd, *As I Live and Breathe* (New York: Random House, 1969).
2. *Ibid*, author's note.
3. "The Word of God" in *The Interpreter's One-Volume Commentary on the Bible*, ed. Charles M. Laymon (Nashville: Abingdon Press, 1971), p. 996.
4. This is the priestly account. The title for God is "God Almighty" (Hebrew "El Shaddai"). This is the same title found in Exod. 6:2-3 where God speaks to Moses concerning the deliverance of his people from Egypt and recalls his appearance to Abraham, Isaac, and Jacob.

II. NARRATIVE WRITERS WITH A MESSAGE

1. W. F. Albright, *From Stone Age to Christianity*, 2nd ed. (Baltimore: John Hopkins Press, 1957), pp. 64-70.
2. See the excellent historical survey of these matters in Samuel Sandmel, *The Hebrew Scriptures* (New York: Alfred A. Knopf, 1963), pp. 324-39.
3. Where several authors or redactors are involved under each designation, scholars sometimes refer to them by such symbols as J ^{1}, J ^{2}, J ^{3}, etc., and similarly for the other letters. The assigned dates do not suggest that the tradition originated at that time; much of it was considerably older.
4. Another interpretation is that it was Solomon himself who encouraged the Yahwist author to put the folklore of the nation into writing.
5. For a significant description of the origin, development, and responsibilities of the priesthood, see the article "Priests and Levites" in *The Interpreter's Dictionary of the Bible* (Nashville: Abingdon Press, 1962), III, 876 ff.
6. The Babylonian creation myth, *Enuma Elish*, has a number of similarities to the priestly account. It is polytheistic, however, and lacks the moral and spiritual tone of the biblical counterpart.
7. See p. 54 where the reading of the law by Ezra is interpreted.
8. The Yahwist also gives an older tradition concerning the Passover (12:21-27). Being less ritual-minded, he includes fewer details.

III. HISTORIANS BEAR WITNESS

1. The Jewish canon lists Josh., Judg., I and II Sam., and I and II Kings as the Former Prophets. English Bibles include I and II Chron., Ezra, and Neh. among the historical books. Ruth and Esther are narrative history or historical fiction.
2. G. Ernest Wright, "Historical Knowledge and Revelation" in *Translating and Understanding the Bible*, ed. Harry Thomas Frank and William L. Reed (Nashville: Abingdon Press, 1970), p. 299.

3. This has also been called "didactic history" because of its teaching values, and "kerygmatic history" because of its preaching message.
4. Paul Tillich, *The Protestant Era* (Chicago: The University of Chicago Press, 1948), p. 22.
5. It has been suggested that the core of the account belonged to the E source, but in its present form it represents D material. The building of an altar by Joshua on Mount Ebal where the covenant was ratified (Josh. 8:30-35) may be a parallel to the Shechem account.
6. Possibly ceremonial blessings were also given, as well as curses. Even ritual involving sacrificial animals and a sacred meal with an exchange of gifts was a possibility. These were customary on such occasions (Josh. 8:30-35; Gen. 15:9-17; 21:27-30; 26:30).
7. *Halford Luccock Treasury,* ed. Robert E. Luccock (Nashville: Abingdon Press, 1963), p. 108.
8. This survey comes from the D editors of Judges. For other such interpretations see Judges 3:7-14; 4:1-3; and 10:6-16.
9. The judges, during this rugged period (the Iron Age, *ca.* 1200 B.C.) following the entering of Canaan, were not lawyers but leaders raised up from the people largely because of their military prowess. After the victory they would usually return to private life.

IV. HISTORIANS INTERPRET THE MONARCHY

1. Harry M. Buck raises the question as to whether the people in asking for a king were rejecting Samuel for Saul. He suggests that possibly Samuel himself may have had dynastic ambitions "which were thwarted." See *People of the Lord* (New York: Macmillan, 1966), p. 60.
2. For a sympathetic interpretation of Saul's mental breakdown see Robert Browning's poem *Saul.* It is more poetical than historical but full of insight.
3. W. F. Albright in *Archaeology and the Religion of Israel,* 4th ed. (Baltimore: Johns Hopkins Press, 1956), p. 130, says that " David's kingdom was the one nearest approach in ancient times for the development of an empire in the western horn of the Fertile Crescent."
4. Prior to this there had been a capital set up by David for a short time at Hebron (II Sam. 2:1-7, 11).
5. See p. 37. A study of the origins of the complete Davidic cycle is quite involved. Coming from various sources the tradition is often out of sequence and sometimes contradictory. The Court History of David is also known as the Throne Succession of David.
6. That David's sin and repentance were widely known is clear from the fact that Psalm 51 was identified by the earliest editors as referring to the king's relationship with Bathsheba. The identification, however, lacks historical ground.
7. Verses 41-53 are sometimes regarded as an expansion of an earlier D version of the prayer by a later (second) Deuteronomist editor.
8. Sandmel writes of the date as "either between 350 and 250 or else about 350, continuing to be added to as late as 250." Sandmel, *The Hebrew Scriptures,* p. 479.

9. Compare I Kings 8; II Chron. 5–7.
10. Wellhäusen regarded the "book of the law of Moses" which was read as the completed Pentateuch (JEDP). Because of the description of the Feast of Booths, which was celebrated the next day (8:13-18), however, some conclude that the P specifications do not seem to have been followed.

V. PROPHETS PREACH THE WORD

1. Sixteen books in the Old Testament comprise the prophetic literature. Four of them are called the Major Prophets, usually because they are longer, e.g. Isaiah, Jeremiah, Ezekiel, and Daniel. The remaining twelve are known as the Minor Prophets because of their brevity, e.g. Hosea, Joel, Amos, Obadiah, Jonah, Micah, Nahum, Habakkuk, Zephaniah, Haggai, Zechariah, and Malachi. Daniel is not regarded today as prophetic in the same sense as the others. It is apocalyptic mostly. The Hebrew Scriptures place it among the Writings.
2. Before the time of Amos, who was a literary prophet since he put his oracles into writing, there were the Pre-literary prophets, including such men as Nathan (II Sam. 12), Ahjah (I Kings 11), Elijah (I Kings 17 ff), and Elisha (I Kings 19:19 ff). These men did not write down their own messages. Their deeds are recorded in the works of the historians.
3. See chapter 1, p. 16. We will not usually distinguish between the several Isaiahs in our quotations: I Isaiah, chapters 1–39; II Isaiah, chapters 40–55; III Isaiah, chapters 56–66.
4. Yehezkel Kaufmann, *The Religion of Israel,* translated and abridged by Moshe Greenberg (Chicago: The University of Chicago Press, 1960), p. 101.
5. For a detailed analysis of prophetic speech, See Clauss Westermann, *Basic Forms of Prophetic Speech,* trans. Hugh Clayton White (Philadelphia: Westminster Press, 1967).
6. For other illustrations of Ezekiel's graphic acted parables, see 4:1-3; 4:4-8; 4:9-15; 24:15-24; 37:15-17.
7. Because of verse 7 in this passage (Mic. 6-8), where child sacrifice is mentioned, a date during the reign of Manasseh (II Kings 21:6) is preferred by some scholars. This would place it later than the time of Micah. Others regard the reign of Ahaz as a possibility (II Kings 16:3). That would make Micah's period likely, as well as his authorship of this important independent fragment.
8. Arnold Toynbee, *An Historian's Approach to Religion* (New York: Oxford University Press, 1956), p. v.
9. *Ibid.,* p. 15.
10. See chapters 3 and 4.
11. See John Bright, *The Kingdom of God* (Nashville: Abingdon Press, 1953), pp. 45 ff, 156 ff.

VI. PSALMISTS SING OF GOD AND MAN

1. Martin Luther, *Preface to the German Psalter,* 1528 (italics mine).
2. Sigmund Mowinckel, *The Psalms in Israel's Worship* (Nashville: Abingdon Press, 1967), pp. 7 ff. Note Psalm 150.
3. *Ibid,* pp. 98-99.
4. Elmer Leslie, *The Psalms* (Nashville: Abingdon Press, 1949), pp. 5-6.
5. A penetrating discussion of the origin and authorship of the psalms may be found in Arthur Weiser, *The Psalms,* trans. Herbert Hartwell (Philadelphia: Westminster Press, 1962), pp. 91 ff.
6. For a contrary view urging that we resist an early dating, see Georg Fohrer, *Introduction to the Old Testament,* trans. David E. Green (Nashville: Abingdon Press, 1968), pp. 283-84.
7. Consult the article "The Literary Forms of the Old Testament" by Dorothea Ward Harvey in *The Interpreter's One-Volume Commentary on the Bible,* pp. 107 ff.
8. Herman Gunkel, *Die Psalmen and Einletung in die Psalmen,* Göttingen, Germany, 1933. A translation of this listing in English with an indication of psalms under each category may be found in Walter Harrelson, *Interpreting the Old Testament* (New York: Holt, Rinehart and Winston, 1964), p. 409.
9. Leslie, *The Psalms,* 1949, p. 37.

VII. WISE MEN CHART THE WAY OF WISDOM

1. Gerhard von Rad, *Wisdom in Israel* (Nashville: Abingdon Press, 1973).
2. For a definitive survey of this body of what has been called "international wisdom," see William McKane, *Proverbs* (Philadelphia: Westminster Press, 1970, pp. 51-208).
3. Book III of Proverbs (22:17–24:22) is thought to be patterned after the Egyptian Book of Wisdom, i.e. "The Instruction of *Amen-em-Opet"* (*ca.* 1000 B.C. and before). These stress what a teacher would say to his pupil, perhaps even to his son, as he instructed him in his responsibilities.
4. Additional listings could include psalms 49, 34, 37, and 112. These classifications are not absolute and depend upon how the interpreter reads the psalm, including the setting he envisages.
5. These Egyptian proverbs are also translated by J. B. Pritchard, ed., *Ancient Near Eastern Texts* (Princeton: Princeton University Press, 1950), pp. 421-25.
6. William M. Elliott, Jr., *Coming to Terms with Life.* Taken from Charles L. Wallis, *A Treasury of Sermon Illustrations* (Nashville: Abingdon Press, 1950), p. 269.
7. Thornton Wilder, *The Angel That Troubled the Waters.*
8. Hugh Anderson, "The Book of Job" in *The Interpreter's One-Volume Commentary on the Bible,* p. 241.
9. The prose section with which the Book of Job closes represents God as rewarding Job because of his faithfulness. It does not reach the high plateau of faith that crowns the poetic section.
10. R. B. Y. Scott, *Proverbs-Ecclesiastes,* Anchor Bible (Garden City, N.Y.: Doubleday, 1965), p. 191.

VIII. GOSPEL WRITERS ANNOUNCE GOOD NEWS

1. Klaus Koch in *The Growth of the Biblical Tradition* (New York: Scribner's, 1971), pp. 54 ff, urges the use of the term "transmission history" for this study, and stresses the connection between the history of the transmission of biblical materials and their historicity.
2. George A. Buttrick, *Sermons Preached in a University Church* (Nashville: Abingdon Press, 1959), p. 7.
3. Papias in Eusebius, *Ecclesiastical History, III,* 39, 15-16.
4. Charles M. Laymon, *Christ in the New Testament* (Nashville: Abingdon Press, 1958), p. 224.
5. Irenaeus, *Against Heresies,* III, 1.1.
6. Papias in Eusebius, *Ecclesiastical History,* III, 39. 15. This view is not accepted by all scholars today, but remains the prevailing judgment. The identity of the author is not an issue in the contention of my book that the Gospel writers were in a very real sense preachers.
7. See Anchor Bible Commentary on Matthew by W. F. Albright and C. S. Mann (Garden City, N. Y.: Doubleday, 1971), especially the section on the "Old Testament Background of Matthew's Gospel," LIV ff. Christological framework, the use of numbers, the example of Qumran commentaries, etc. are considered in explaining the structure and arrangement of Matthew.
8. Eusebius, *Ecclesiastical History,* III, 4.6 identifies Matthew with the tax collector and disciple of Jesus. The Gospel itself makes no such claim. For a contrary view with considerable documentation see W. G. Kümmel's reedited edition of the Introduction to the New Testament by Paul Feine and Johannes Behm (Nashville: Abingdon Press, 1965), pp. 84-86. The author is here regarded as a Greek-speaking Jewish Christian of considerable rabbinic knowledge who "assimilated the sayings of Jesus to Jewish views."
9. Note the repetition of the statement: "And when Jesus had finished these sayings" at five points in the Gospel (Matt. 7:28; 11:1; 13:53; 19:1; 26:1).
10. John Henry Jowett, *The Preacher, His Life and Work* (New York: Harper, 1912), p. 118.
11. Col. 4:14; Philem. 24; II Tim. 4:11.
12. The Acts of the Apostles, which Luke also wrote, further highlights the fact that the church was not anti-government. As a missionary Paul was not disloyal to the state and on occasion pridefully asserted his rights as a Roman citizen (16:35-40; 22:25-29; 25:10-12).
13. Taken from the *Halford Luccock Treasury,* p. 147. Originally written in *Communicating the Gospel* (New York: Harper, 1954). Italics mine.
14. To some extent there are similarities of terminology and conception between the Gospel of John and the Dead Sea Scrolls. Does this suggest that the Fourth Gospel should be dated much earlier so that it could even be the First Gospel? The so-called Gnosticism of the Scrolls may provide the background for the Gospel of John rather than that of the Greeks. This, of course, remains suppositional.

15. For a perceptive consideration of the authorship of the Gospel of John see Charles H. Dodd, *The Interpretation of the Fourth Gospel* (London: Cambridge University Press, 1953). Also, Raymond E. Brown, *The Gospel According to John*, I-XII, The Anchor Bible Series (Garden City, N. Y.: Doubleday, 1966).
16. Rudolf Bultmann, *The Gospel of John*, trans. G. R. Beasley-Murray, R. W. N. Hoare, and J. K. Riches (Philadelphia: Westminster Press, 1971), p. 222.

IX. JESUS CAME PREACHING

1. The italics used in this chapter have been added by the author.
2. Reference has already been made in this book to the distinction between the teaching message (*didache*) and the preaching message (*kerygma*) in the Bible. We regard this as a valid distinction, but in the case of Jesus' personal activity as seen in the Gospels, it is difficult to apply. Is the Sermon on the Mount kerygma or didache? See the collection of essays *The Historical Jesus and the Kerygmatic Christ*, ed. Carl E. Braaten and Roy A. Harrisville (Nashville: Abingdon Press, 1964). It is our view that the Gospel record which regards Jesus as a preacher and a teacher is not mythological. These functions were historical in his ministry.
3. Alexander V. G. Allen, *Life and Letters of Phillips Brooks*, three vols. (New York: E. P. Dutton, 1901), II, 143.
4. Matt. 5:15-16 and Luke 11:33; Matt. 5:25-56 and Luke 12:57-59; Matt. 6:9-13 and Luke 11:2-4; Matt. 7:22-23 and Luke 13:26-27.
5. These were to be men of leisure (Batlanim) so that they would have sufficient time to give to the needs of the synagogue. See the Talmudic tractate Sanhedrin 1.6.
6. Bornkamm emphasizes the importance of the synagogue in an area remote from Jerusalem and the temple. Galilee, where Jesus grew up, was such an area: "It is . . . easily understood that through the physical separation from the temple, the synagogue became here the centre of Judaism." Gunther Bornkamm, *Jesus of Nazareth*, trans. Irene and Fraser McLuskey with James M. Robinson (New York: Harper 1959), p. 42.
7. Jeremias regards the parables as unique—"something entirely new" with Jesus and says: "In all the rabbinic literature, not one single parable has come down to us from the period before Jesus." Joachim Jeremias, *Rediscovering the Parables* (New York: Scribner's, 1966), p. 10.
8. C. H. Dodd, *The Parables of the Kingdom* (New York: Scribner's, 1961) chapter 4. See also W. O. E. Oesterly, *The Gospel Parables in the Light of their Jewish Background* (New York: Macmillan 1936), selected readings.
9. David Flusser, *Jesus* (New York: Herder and Herder, 1969), p. 47.
10. Because of the nature of our sources, and the fact that there must be many of Jesus' statements that have been lost, it would be unwise to draw major conclusions from the references noted. Yet they do say something about Jesus' use of his Bible in preaching as far as our records are concerned.

11. See *Halford Luccock Treasury*, p. 401.
12. Scholars have taken various views of Jesus' messiahship as he himself thought of it. Wrede in 1901 wrote that the church ascribed messiahship to Jesus in view of the resurrection; Bultmann held that Jesus' life and work were non-messianic. Craig considered Jesus to have regarded himself as the Messiah but made no claims as he waited for God to make it known; Schweitzer, and others who followed him, believed that Jesus identified himself with the apocalyptic Son of man. See the notation of these and other views in Laymon, *Christ in the New Testament*, pp. 146-50.

X. THE EARLY CHURCH COMMUNICATES THE TRUTH

1. Floyd V. Filson, *A New Testament History* (Philadelphia: Westminster Press, 1964), p. 172.
2. A careful analysis of these matters is found in Henry J. Cadbury, "The Summaries in Acts," *The Beginnings of Christianity* (New York: Macmillan, 1920-1933), V, 392-402.
3. In the Gospel of John it is the risen Christ who bestows the Holy Spirit first upon the disciples (20:22). As Bultmann says in his commentary on this gospel: ". . . the Risen Jesus bestows the Spirit on the disciples through his breath . . . Easter and Pentecost therefore fall together." Rudolf Bultmann, *The Gospel of John*, p. 692.
4. See Bright, *The Kingdom of God*, pp. 45 ff, 156 ff for an illuminating discussion of the Day of the Lord expectation.
5. Rudolf Bultmann, *Theology of the New Testament*, trans. Kendrick Grobel (New York: Scribner's, 1951), I, 44.
6. The reference to Jesus as God's "servant" suggests Isaiah 52:13–53;12 where the suffering servant is introduced. In calling him "the Holy and Righteous One," Peter may have had in mind Isaiah 53:11 *b* where it is said of the servant that "by his knowledge shall the righteous one, my servant, make many to be accounted righteous." The reference to Jesus as "the Author of life," however, takes us to passages in Hebrews 2:10 and 12:2, rather than to the Old Testament.
7. The reaction in the church against Peter's baptizing a Gentile seems to suggest that this was an innovation. Yet already Phillip had preached a revival at a city in Samaria (Sebaste?) where multitudes responded. Because of its city-wide influence and location, numbers of Gentiles must have been baptized along with Jewish converts. And all received the Holy Spirit after Peter came down from Jerusalem to lay his hands upon them (Acts 8:14-17). As Hans Conzelmann in *History of Primitive Christianity* (p. 66) states: "In reality there was no such single act which solved the problem once and for all." Trans. John E. Steely (Nashville: Abingdon Press, 1973).
8. C. H. Dodd, in commenting on this and other similar sermonic summaries in Acts such as we have been examining, says: "If these forms of *kerygma* [preaching message] in Acts may be accepted as repre-

senting with reasonable fidelity the general type of early preaching, as I believe they may, then the gospel narratives . . . would readily serve the purpose of exemplifying or illustrating the statements made in general terms in the *kerygma.* The 'concise' narratives such as Peter's sermon at Caesarea would be precisely . . . 'paradigms' for the use of the preacher." C. H. Dodd, *More New Testament Studies* (Grand Rapids: Eerdmans, 1968), p. 124.

9. Acts notes that Stephen performed "signs and wonders" (6:8) as well as preached. Is there a contradiction here that calls for an additional document that somehow became associated with the source stressing his preaching ministry? Note also the double narrative in which the charge against Stephen is repeated twice (vss. 9-11 and 12-14), and the possibly double account of his stoning (7:54-58*a* and 7:58*b*-60).

10. The question has been raised by some scholars as to whether this really is Stephen's own sermon, as well as to its historical accuracy. Could it not have been an insert? Yet, Cadbury and Lake point out that it is non-Pauline, for it does not deal with Paul's Judaistic controversies. The use of one's defense time to make a speech was typical in that day. Therefore it could be from Stephen himself or what early Christians, before Paul, assigned to him. See Jackson and Lake, *The Beginnings of Christianity* (New York: Macmillan, 1920-1933), IV, 69-70.

11. *The Interpreter's Bible* (Nashville: Abingdon Press, 1954), IX, 92.

XI. PAUL PROCLAIMS SALVATION

1. Hans Conzelmann suggests that Paul preached for at least ten years in Syria/Cilicia and that Acts summarizes some experiences in this area in the record of the first missionary journey as reported in Acts 13-14. See his *History of Primitive Christianity,* pp. 81-82.

2. The specific imprisonment is uncertain. Paul was in prison probably two years at Caesarea (Acts 24:27). Later he was under house arrest in Rome (Acts 28:16, 30-31). His mention in Philippians of the praetorian guard (1:13) and also Caesar's household (4:22) most likely argue for a Roman imprisonment. Some scholars, however, favor Ephesus; one reason among others is Paul's statement in I Corinthians (15:32) in which he says that he had fought with wild beasts at Ephesus. This, of course, may be a metaphorical remark. Ephesus as the site of the imprisonment would place Philippians in the middle of Paul's career.

3. There is an increasing interest in Gnosticism as it provides a background and even a tool for interpreting Christian writing, in the New Testament. A translation of Walter Schmithal's *Gnosticism in Corinth* opens the way for similar possibilities in approaching other letters of Paul. Trans. John E. Steely (Nashville: Abingdon Press, 1971). See pp. 25-86 especially.

4. James D. Smart, *Doorway to a New Age* (New York: Joint Commission on Education and Cultivation, Board of Missions, United Methodist Church, 1972), p. 153.

5. I and II Thessalonians, Galatians, I and II Corinthians, Romans, Philippians, and Philemon are generally held as Pauline. Colossians is most usually but not always so regarded. Ephesians is often questioned as being wholly Pauline, as are also I and II Timothy and Titus. Genuine Pauline passages, however, are usually thought to exist in this latter group.

6. The validity of Paul's speeches in the book of Acts has been questioned even as have been the sermons of Peter, because of the similarities between them, the absence of stenographers or electronic recording equipment, and the practice in that day of authors ghost writing speeches for their characters. Thucydides says that when he wrote speeches he tried to employ the language and sense which he thought the speaker would use. He adhered as closely as possible to the general sense of what was actually said (*History of Peloponnesian War* 1. 22). In this connection see also H. J. Cadbury, *The Book of Acts in History* (New York: Harper, 1955), pp. 128-29. Verbal accuracy is too much to insist upon in these areas. It is the ideas that matter most; if those in the speeches parallel what we know about the thinking of the speaker from other verified sources we are on sounder ground. Paul's ideas in his sermons in Acts on the whole can be paralleled in his epistles. They also are psychologically pertinent to the situations in which they were preached. Undoubtedly Luke tooled them for the occasion, but this is not the same thing as inventing them.

7. Some scholars think that the Areopagus was the judicial court where a friendly hearing took place. When Paul's crowd left him it was because of their lack of interest in his reference to judgment and the Resurrection rather than because of legal involvements (17:32).

8. The author of the first of these quotations is not actually known, but its sentiments are typical of the pantheism preached by the Stoics. Epimenides, "a semimythical" Cretan has been suggested. The reference to man as God's offspring most likely comes from the *Phaenomena* of Aratus (born 310 B.C.), which the Stoics may have been quoting to support their philosophy.

9. O. T. background verses which suggest ideas for this paeon of praise: "For who has known . . ." see Isa. 40:13; "Or who has given a gift . . ." see Job 35:7 or 41:11. For the final statement of praise see Ps. 73:17.

10. P. 136.

11. Frank W. Beare, *Saint Paul and His Letters* (Nashville: Abingdon Press, 1962), p. 19.

12. In *From Jesus to Paul,* Joseph Klausner, expresses his belief that Paul intended for these letters to be "more or less public," and that this lifts "these Epistles above the level of private letters." (New York: Macmillan, 1943), p. 235.

13. Chapter 16 is probably a fragment of a correspondence with the church at Ephesus. Note verses 3-4, 5, 7, 17-20. Could Paul have sent a copy of Romans to Ephesus and appended this finale for their benefit, as some scholars have suggested? What he said in Romans had broad universal significance.

14. Such references as the following spell out this salvation: 3:21-26; 5:8-11; 7:7-25.

15. An exceedingly thorough study on love in the New Testament is Victor Paul Furnish's *Love Command in the New Testament* (Nashville: Abingdon Press, 1972). In regard to I Corinthians 13, in particular see pages 95, 99, 100, 111-13, 121, 128, 181, 187. Paul uses here the word *agape*, which is the characteristic New Testament word for love. It stands for a love that is freely given, not earned or deserved, but graciously poured forth on the one who receives it. See the appendix in the above book for an excellent delineation on love as *agape*, pp. 219-31.

XII. THE LATER CHURCH CONFRONTS ITS AGE

1. I Peter is classed with what we call the General Epistles or the Catholic Epistles. These include I and II Peter, James, I, II, and III John, and Jude. They are not directed to a specific church by name, but apply generally and deal with persecution, heresy, disunity, and immorality.
2. Another reason for denying this letter to Peter the apostle is that it seems to contain Pauline references when 2:6, 8 is compared with Romans 9:32-33. Would Peter have copied from Paul?
3. Hans Conzelmann regards the persecutions in I Peter as occurring under Domitian: "I Peter, Revelation, and I Clement all are aware of persecution. These writings may very well have arisen in this time." *History of Primitive Christianity*, p. 130.
4. But see the references to the suffering and death of Jesus in I Peter 3:18; 4:1, 13; 5:1.
5. The reference here to suffering as a Christian has been pivotal for some in dating I Peter. They point out that Nero's persecution of the Christians was not because of their religious identification, but because of the fact that he was blaming them for the burning of Rome. In Domitian's time, however, the persecution was the result of their refusal to practice emperor worship because they were Christians. But Archibald Hunter says: "There is absolutely nothing in the language to compel such a conclusion . . . such suffering was no new thing: in the earliest days of the faith we read that the apostles rejoiced 'that they were accounted worthy to suffer dishonor for the name' (Acts 5:41)." *The Interpreter's Bible* (Nashville: Abingdon Press, 1957), XII, p. 145.
6. H. T. Andrews in *The Abingdon Bible Commentary* (Nashville: Abingdon Press, 1929), p. 1298, argues for Hebraic Christians. But T. H. Robinson favors a group in the Hellenistic world, similar to those to whom the Revelation to John was addressed. See his *Epistle to the Hebrews*, Moffatt Commentary Series (New York: Harper, 1933), p. xvii.
7. Both of these suggestions (Rome and Ephesus) are offered by A. E. J. Rawlinson in *Christ in the Gospels* (London: Longmans, Green, 1949), p. 176. The Epistle of Clement of Rome (*ca.* A.D. 96) is the first to quote it. But its thought patterns fit Ephesus also.
8. H. T. Andrews calls this the "first great attempt that was made to explain Christianity in terms of Platonic philosophy." (*The Abingdon Bible Commentary*, p. 1295.)

9. See the Introduction to the Revelation to John in the *Interpreter's One-Volume Commentary on the Bible*, pp. 945 ff. The author is S. MacLean Gilmour. *The Interpreter's Bible*, XII, 356 ff, contains an excellent discussion on authorship written by Martin Rist.

10. The word "apocalypse" comes from the Greek word meaning "unveiling," usually with reference to the future. Apocalyptic writing appeared in tense times when a cataclysmic deliverance from heaven seemed man's only hope. It makes use of vision, symbols, and highly dramatic expressions. Recommended reading here includes E. F. Scott, *The Book of Revelation* (New York: Scribner's, 1940); J. A. T. Robinson, *Jesus and His Coming* (Nashville: Abingdon Press, 1958); and the author's *Book of Revelation* (Nashville: Abingdon Press, 1960).

11. See the discussion of this subject in Feine, Behm, and Kümmel's, *Introduction to the New Testament*, p. 286.

12. Because of this character, James the brother of Jesus has been suggested as its author. There is no great tradition or acceptance as such behind this idea. The book omits allusions to Jesus which he surely would have made had he been his brother.

13. Feine, Behm, and Kümmel, *Introduction to the New Testament*, p. 291: "His [the author of the letter to James] familiarity with the LXX [Greek translation of the O. T. known as the Septuagint], his literary language, and his designation of the Christians as people of the diaspora (1:1) speak against the supposition that the author was a Palestinian."

Indexes

INDEX OF SCRIPTURE

INDEX OF SUBJECTS

Dodd, C. H., 119
The Apostolic Preaching and Its Development, 100
Domitian, Emperor, 104, 153

E. *See* Elohist authors
Early church
preaching in, 124-25
Ecclesiastes, book of, 96-97
Edinburgh, University of, 34, 65
Egypt; Egyptians, 84, 87, 131
Elijah (prophet), 121
Elisha (prophet), 121
Elohist authors, 24, 27-30, 54
Emmaus, 110
Ephesus, 104
Epicurus, 139
Ethan the Ezrahite, 76
Euphrates River, 60
Eusebius
Ecclesiastical History, 99
Eve, 26
Exile, Babylonian, 16, 24, 31, 33, 51, 53, 56, 59, 60, 77, 94, 115
Exodus, book of, 121. *See also* Pentateuch
Ezekiel (prophet), 16, 18, 57, 60, 115
Ezra (priest), 54
Ezra, book of, 51

Filson, Floyd V.
A New Testament History, 124
Flood, The
Yahwist account, 27
Flusser, David, 120
Form criticism, 98
Fourth Gospel. *See* John, Gospel of
Gamaliel, 135
Genesis, book of, 121. *See also* Pentateuch
Gideon, 42-43
Gilgamesh Epic, 27
Gnosticism, 107, 134
God
Bible as voice of, 15-19
covenant with Abraham, 26, 32-33
Day of the Lord, 68-70, 126, 127
God's love in Christ, 141-42
history and, 37, 65-67
Israel's kingship and, 45
kingdom of, in Jesus' preaching, 121-23
obedience to, 46-47
Prophets and, 55-56

God (*continued*)
righteousness of, 64-65
universalism of, in Luke's Gospel, 105-6
Godspell, 13
Goodspeed, Edgar J., 13
Gospel writers
"Gospel" defined, 98
portrait of Jesus, 108-11
preaching message of, 99-101, 111
Grant, Frederick, 98

Haggai, 52
Hallam, Arthur, 75
Hebrews, Letter to, 149-52
Hegel, G. W. F., 41
Heman the Ezrahite, 76
Herod, King, 105
Herodotus, 22
Hilkiah (priest), 38
History, 21
biblical historians, 35-37
communist view, 41-42
"cycles of apostasy" view (Judges), 42-44
cyclical view, 41
Deuteronomic historians, 38-44
evolutionary view, 41
God in, 21-22, 65-67
moral predication of, 43
philosophies of, 41-44
salvation history, 36-37
theories of kingship in biblical narratives, 45-54
Hitler, Adolf, 68
Hope
Psalm 42 as liturgy of, 81-82
Hosea (prophet), 16, 28, 57, 59, 61-62, 64, 65, 67, 91
Hosea, book of, 121
Hughes, Bishop Edwin Holt, 133

Instruction of Amen-em-Opet, The, 92
Isaac, 16, 40, 121, 128
sacrifice of, 28-29
Isaiah (prophet), 18, 57-58, 62, 63, 65, 66, 67, 69, 70. *See also* Second Isaiah
Isaiah, book of, 120

J. *See* Yahwist authors
Jacob, 16, 40, 121, 128
James, Letter of, 154-56
Jebusites, 47
Jefferson, Thomas, 68

William Jessup University
Library
333 Sunset Blvd.
Rocklin, Ca 95765